TAKE A
HIKE

Family Walks
in the
Rochester, NY
Area

Copyright © 2010 by Rich and Sue Freeman

First edition: 1997 (ISBN: 0-9656974-6-0)
Second edition: 2000: (ISBN: 0-9656974-7-9)
Third edition: 2010 (ISBN: 978-1-930480-14-8)

Published in the United States of America by Footprint Press, Inc.

Cover Design by Michael Lynch, www.bookcoverdesign.com

Maps by Rich Freeman

Pictures by Rich & Sue Freeman

Back cover photos:
   Rich Freeman at MacKay Wildlife Refuge
   Turtles on a log at Brighton Town Park

ISBN 10 digit: 1-930480-14-8
ISBN 13 digit: 978-1-930480-14-8

Manufactured in the United States of America

TAKE A
HIKE

Family Walks
in the
Rochester, NY
Area

303 Pine Glen Court, Englewood, FL 34223
www.footprintpress.com

Footprint Press publishes a variety of outdoor recreation guidebooks. See a complete list and order form at the back of this book and at web site www.footprintpress.com. We also publish a free, blog called *New York Outdoors*. To sign up visit: http://newyorkoutdoors.wordpress.com

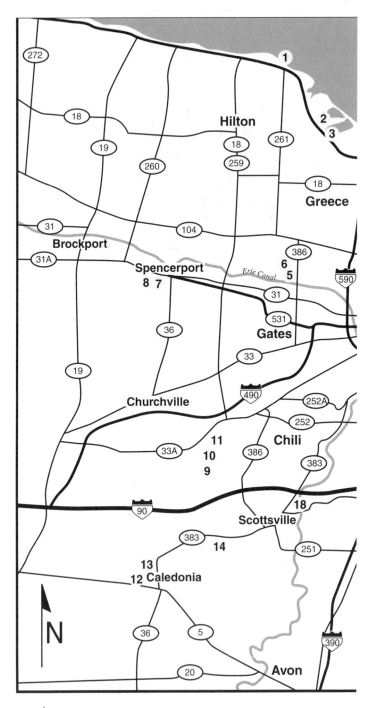

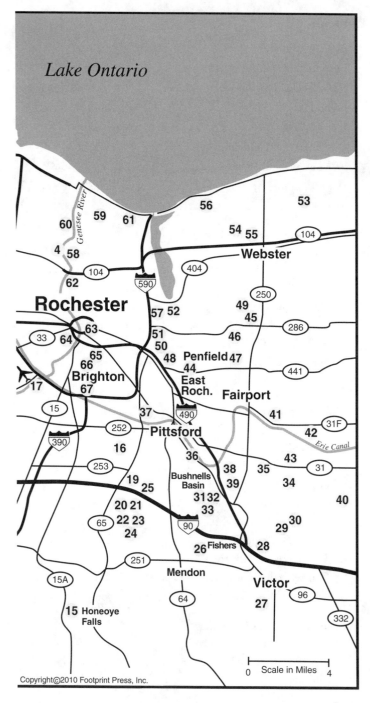

Lake Ontario

Genesee River

Rochester

Brighton

Pittsford

Fairport

Webster

Penfield

East Roch.

Bushnells Basin

Fishers

Mendon

Victor

Honeoye Falls

Erie Canal

59 61
60
4 58
62
57 52
63
64 65 66 67
33
17
15
37
252
16
253
19 25
20 21 22 23 24
65
251
15A
15

56
54 55
49 45
46
51 50
48 44 47
41
42
36
38 39 35 43 34
31 32 33
26 28
29 30
27
40

53
104
404
250
286
441
31F
31
96
332
590
490
90
390

Copyright©2010 Footprint Press, Inc.

0   Scale in Miles   4

5

Contents

Acknowledgments

The research, writing, production, and promotion of a book such as this is never a solitary adventure. *Take A Hike* came into being because of the assistance of many wonderful people who freely shared their knowledge, experience, resources, thoughts, and time. Many people directed us to choice trails, reviewed our maps and descriptions, supplied historical tidbits, and often are responsible for the existence and maintenance of the trails. We extend our heartfelt thanks to them all. Each in his or her own way is responsible for making the Rochester area a better place to live and, most of all, a community rich with the spirit of collaboration for the betterment of all. This is what ensures quality of life within a community.

Our latest assistant was Tom Andrews. He acted as our eyes and legs and hiked quite a few of the trails, providing us with detailed updates for this edition. Thanks Tom.

Introduction

Wow, what a ride this has been. In 1997 we issued the original *Take A Hike* book and wondered if the Rochester community would show any interest. We worked hard to get the word out and were rewarded with a warm reception. Our greatest thrill was at book signings when people would come up to us and glowingly describe how the book had inspired them, either solo or as part of a group, to begin an exercise program based on hiking each of the trails. Now that you've been inspired to begin, keep hiking. This 3rd edition has additional new trails to explore.

If you're new to the Rochester area, there's no better way to learn your way around than by using this book as your guide. It will introduce you to our rich history and lead you to explore our diverse natural beauty.

Besides, taking a hike or a short walk is good for you. In as little as one hour you can do your body a favor – stretch your legs, raise your heart rate, and decrease your stress level. Hiking is a perfect exercise to balance today's hectic lifestyle.

Rochester and the surrounding towns are a treasure trove of great walks. The geographic terrain varies greatly and wildlife is abundant. The city and towns have had the vision to create parks and save wetlands, many with trails. The Rochester area is unique in its level of volunteerism in the establishment and maintenance of hiking trails. Few other cities have local trail groups like Rochester. The trail groups all welcome volunteers and new members. We encourage everyone to join and help build and preserve trails for future generations to enjoy.

Most trails listed in this book are free and open to the public. A few require a small admission fee or request a donation. They are clearly noted in the heading to each trail beside the term "Admission." You do not have to be a member of the sponsoring group to enjoy any of the trails.

If you find inaccurate information or substantially different conditions (after all, things do change), please send a note detailing your findings to:

Footprint Press, 303 Pine Glen Court, Englewood, FL 34223
or e-mail us: info@footprintpress.com

How To Use This Book

We have clustered the hikes into five groups using the city of Rochester as the core and working in a counter clockwise spiral from the northwest, around the city. All the walks are found in Monroe County or the northwest corner of Ontario County — the Rochester suburban area:

Walks Northwest of Rochester
Walks Southwest of Rochester
Walks Southeast of Rochester
Walks Northeast of Rochester
Walks in Central Rochester

An overall map showing the locations of all the trails, by trail number, can be found on pages 4 and 5.

There's a major hiking trail in Rochester that you won't find in this book. The Erie Canalway Trail runs for over 90 miles from Lockport to Newark and is used year-round by walkers, bikers, joggers, in-line skaters, and cross-country skiers. Maps and trail descriptions for this trail (any many other walkable trails) can be found in the guidebooks *Take Your Bike- Family Rides in the Rochester Area* and *Take Your Bike - Family Rides in New York's Finger Lakes Region*.

Where possible, we have designated hikes that go in a loop to let you see as much as possible without backtracking. You can easily begin and end in one location and not worry about finding transportation back to the beginning. The indexes at the back list trails by a variety of criteria. Refer to them, to quickly zero in on trails that suit your purposes.

Approximate hiking times are given, but of course this depends on your speed. If you stop to watch the wildlife, enjoy the views, or read the descriptive plaques, it will take you longer than the time given. You'll notice that many of the hikes also have shortcuts or are connected to other trails that allow you to adjust your time on the trail.

Each hike in this guide is mapped. The maps are easy to understand so everyone can be comfortable heading down an unknown trail. On most of the maps, you'll find a small inset map. This gives a broader picture and lets you visually locate the trail relative to major towns and roads.

We found people were keeping notes in the margins of their original *Take A Hike* books, so we've added a section at the end of each trail for you to log the date visited and any notes you may want to jot down about your experience on a specific trail.

Once you've explored all these trails, pick up a copy of the guidebook *Take A Hike - Family Walks in New York's Finger Lakes Region* and keep on hiking.

Happy Trails!

Legend

At the beginning of each trail listing, you will find a map and description with the following information:

Location: The park, nature center, or town the trail is in.

Directions: How to find the trailhead parking area from a major road or town.

Alternative Parking: Other parking locations with access to the trail. Use these if you want to shorten or lengthen your hike by starting or stopping at a spot other than the designated endpoint.

Hiking Time: Approximate time to hike at a comfortable pace, including time to enjoy the views.

Length: The round-trip length of the hike in miles (unless noted as one-way).

Difficulty:

(1 boot) easy hiking, generally level trail

(2 boots) rolling hills, gradual grades on trail

(3 boots) gentle climbing required to follow the trail

(4 boots) some strenuous climbing required

Surface: The materials that make up the trail surface for the major portion of the hike.

Trail Markings: Markings used to designate the trails in this book vary widely. Some trails are not marked at all but can be followed by cleared or worn paths. This doesn't pose a problem for the hiker as long as there aren't many intersecting, unmarked paths. Other trails are well marked with either signs, blazes, or markers, and sometimes a combination of all three. Marking is done by the official group that maintains the trail.

Signs – wooden, plastic or metal signs with instructions in words or pictures.

Blazes – painted markings on trees showing where the trail goes. Many blazes are rectangular and placed at eye level. Colors may be used to denote different trails. If a tree has twin blazes beside one another, you should proceed cautiously because the trail either turns or another trail intersects.

Sometimes you'll see a section of trees with painted markings which aren't neat geometric shapes. These are probably boundary markers or trees marked for logging. Trail blazes are generally distinct geometric shapes and are placed at eye level.

Markers – small plastic or metal geometric shapes (square, round, triangular) nailed to trees at eye level to show where the trail goes. They also may be colored to denote different trails.

It is likely that at some point you will lose the blazes or markers while following a trail. The first thing to do is stop and look around. See if you can spot a blaze or marker by looking in all directions, including behind you. If not, backtrack until you see a blaze or marker, then proceed forward again, carefully following the markings.

Uses: Each trail has a series of icons depicting the activity or activities allowed on the trail. Jogging is allowed on all trails, as is snowshoeing when snow covers the ground. The icons include:

 Hiking

 Horseback Riding

 Bicycling

 Snowmobiling

 Cross-country Skiing

 Wheelchair Accessible

Contact: The address and phone number of the organization to contact if you would like additional information or if you have questions not answered in this book.

Map Legend

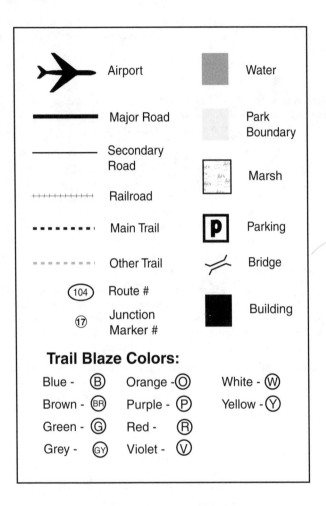

✈	Airport	▨	Water
▬▬▬	Major Road	▨	Park Boundary
───	Secondary Road	▨	Marsh
+++++++++	Railroad		
▪ ▪ ▪ ▪ ▪	Main Trail	P	Parking
▫ ▫ ▫ ▫ ▫	Other Trail	✗	Bridge
(104)	Route #	■	Building
⑰	Junction Marker #		

Trail Blaze Colors:

Blue -	Ⓑ	Orange - Ⓞ		White - Ⓦ	
Brown -	⒝ᴿ	Purple - Ⓟ		Yellow - Ⓨ	
Green -	Ⓖ	Red -	Ⓡ		
Grey -	⒢ʸ	Violet -	Ⓥ		

Directions

In the directions we often tell you to turn left or right. To avoid confusion, in some instances we have noted a compass direction in parentheses according to the following:

(N) = north   (E) = east
(S) = south   (W) = west

Some trails have "Y" or "T" junctions. A "Y" junction indicates one path that turns into two paths. The direction we give is either bear left or bear right. A "T" junction is one path that ends at another. The direction is turn left or turn right.

Guidelines

Any adventure in the outdoors can be inherently dangerous. It's important to watch where you are going and keep an eye on children. Some of these trails are on private property where permission is benevolently granted by the landowners. Please respect the landowners and their property. Follow all regulations posted on signs and stay on the trails. Our behavior today will determine how many of these wonderful trails remain for future generations to enjoy.

Follow "no-trace" ethics whenever you venture outdoors. "No-trace" ethics means that the only thing left behind as evidence of your passing is your footprints. Carry out all trash you carry in. Do not litter. In fact, carry a plastic bag with you and pick up any litter you happen upon along the way. The trails included in this book are intended for day hikes. Please, no camping or fires.

As the trails age and paths become worn, trail work groups sometimes reroute the trails. This helps control erosion and allows vegetation to return. It also means that if a sign or marker doesn't appear as it is described in the book, it's probably because of trail improvement.

Remember:

Take only pictures, leave only footprints.
Please do not pick anything.

Preparations and Safety

You can enhance your time in the outdoors by dressing properly and carrying appropriate equipment. Even for a short day hike, take a small backpack or fanny pack with the following gear:

camera	flashlight
binoculars	insect repellent
compass	water bottle with water
rain gear	nature guidebook(s) of flowers, birds, etc.
snacks	plastic bag to pick up trash

Many of the trails can be muddy. It's best to wear lightweight hiking boots or at least sturdy sneakers.

Walking sticks have been around for centuries, but they are finding new life and new forms in recent years. These sticks can be anything from a branch picked up along the trail to a $200 pair of poles designed with built-in springs and hand-molded grips. Using a walking stick is a good idea, especially in hilly terrain. It can take the pressure off your knees and help you balance when crossing bridges or logs.

Hiking with children is good exercise as well as an opportunity for learning. Use the time to teach children how to read a compass, identify flowers, trees, birds, and animal tracks. You'll find books on each of these subjects in the public library.

Make it fun by taking a different type of gorp for each hike. Gorp (an acronym for Good Old Raisins and Peanuts) is any combination of dried foods that you eat as a snack. Examples are:

1) peanuts, M&M's®, and raisins
2) chocolate morsels, nuts, and granola
3) dried banana chips, sunflower seeds, and carob chips

Get creative and mix any combination of chocolate, carob, dried fruits, nuts, oats, granolas, etc. The bulk food section at your local grocery store is a wealth of ideas. Other fun snacks are marshmallows, popcorn, peanuts in shells, graham crackers, and beef jerky.

When hiking with a child, tie a string on a whistle and have your child wear it as a necklace for safety. Instruct your child to blow the whistle only if he or she is lost.

Dogs Welcome!

Hiking with dogs can be fun because of their keen sense of smell and different perspective on the world. Many times they find things that we would have passed by. They're inquisitive about everything and make excellent companions. But to ensure that your hiking companion enjoys the time outside, you must control your dog. Dogs are required to be leashed on most maintained public trails. The reasons are numerous, but the top ones are to protect dogs, to protect other hikers, and to ensure your pet doesn't chase wildlife. Good dog manners go a long way toward creating goodwill and improving tolerance toward their presence.

58 of the trails listed in this book welcome dogs. Please respect the requirement that dogs be leashed where noted.

The only trails which **prohibit** dogs are:

Trail #	Trail Name
1	Owl Migration Trail
12	Genesee Country Nature Center
16	Tinker Nature Park
21	Birdsong Trail (Mendon Ponds Park)
22	Quaker Pond Trail (Mendon Ponds Park
24	Mendon Grasslands Trail (Mendon Ponds Park)
30	MaryFrances Bluebird Haven
49	Thousand Acre Swamp
59	Helmer Nature Center

Seasons

Most people head into the great outdoors in summer. Temperatures are warm, the days are long, and plants and wildlife are plentiful. Summer is a great time to go hiking. But don't neglect the other seasons. Each season offers a unique perspective, and makes hiking the same trail a totally different adventure. In spring, a time of rebirth, you can watch the leaves unfurl and the spring flowers burst.

Become a leaf peeper in fall. Venture forth onto the trails and take in the colorful splendor of a beautiful fall day. Listen to the rustle of newly fallen leaves under your feet and inhale the unique smell of this glorious season.

The only complication with fall is that it coincides with hunting season. The vast majority of trails in this book are in parks or suburban areas where hunting is not permitted. The only exceptions might be Quinn Oak Openings and Genesee Valley Greenway. Wear blaze orange when hiking in the fall on land that may be used for hunting.

And, finally, winter. It may be cold out, but the leaves are off the trees and the views will never be better. You can more fully appreciate the variety of this area's terrain if you wander out in winter. It is also the perfect time to watch for animal tracks in the snow and test your identification skills. If the snow is deep. it's helpful to wear snowshoes.

Northwest
Section

1

Owl Migration Trail

Location:	Braddock Bay Raptor Research, Manitou Beach Road, Hilton
Directions:	From Lake Ontario State Parkway, exit at Manitou Beach Road. The parking area is on the northeast side of the exit ramp.
Alternate Parking:	None
Hiking Time:	45 minutes
Length:	0.9 mile loop
Difficulty:	
Surface:	Woodchip path and boardwalks
Trail Markings:	None
Uses:	
Dogs:	Pets are NOT allowed
Admission:	Free
Contact:	Braddock Bay Raptor Research 432 Manitou Beach Road, Hilton, NY 14468 www.bbrr.org
	Braddock Bay Bird Observatory PO Box 12876, Rochester, NY 14612 (585) 234-3525 http://www.bbbo.org/
	N.Y.S. D.E.C. Regional Office 6274 Avon-Lima Road Avon, NY 14414 (585) 226-2466

Visit the Owl Migration Trail in the spring or fall to get a close look at owls and hawks as they migrate north. Upwards of 100,000 hawks, eagles, falcons, and vultures migrate over Braddock Bay along Lake Ontario each spring. The birds find it difficult to fly over the cold waters of Lake Ontario and prefer to fly around it. Braddock Bay is located on a point where the shoreline dips south. Because of the dip, birds stop to rest and get concentrated in this area during migration.

This migration of raptors or birds of prey offers a unique opportunity to learn a great deal about the birds. One common research technique is capturing, banding, and releasing the birds.

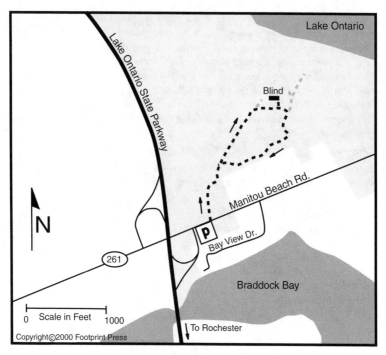

Owl Migration Trail

A hawk-banding blind was built in 1984 and is open for visitation. This is the only banding station in North America with an open door policy. However, you must adhere to the following guidelines, or the policy could change.

Policy Guidelines for the Hawk-Banding Area
- Enter only by the back door via the boardwalk from the main trail.
- When you can see the back of the blind, yell "Clear?" and wait for a response. If there is no answer, wait where you are. No response could mean the operators haven't heard you or they are remaining quiet because a hawk is nearby. Try calling again after 30 seconds. If the response is "No," wait until the operator gives you clearance to come in.
- If no one answers please do not enter the area or touch the nets and traps. Do not go out to the traps without permission.
- Ask permission to photograph or videotape any bird or trap.
- Sometimes the blind can become crowded, and the operator will request either that you take only a short look or that you come back at a later time.

From mid-April through early-June for the spring migration, and again from late-August through mid-October for the fall migration, hawks migrate during the day. Owls migrate at night, sleeping in the pine forest and thickets until evening, when they continue their journey. The trail wraps around and through this small grouping of pine trees allowing the opportunity to view the birds up close if you're lucky. The most common species of owls you will see is the northern saw-whet, but others such as the long-eared, short-eared, and great-horned have been seen here also. Informative signs along the trail teach about the migrating owls and the habitat they prefer. Remember, this area was established to help protect raptors. We are the visitors and should be respectful by being quiet and staying on the established trails.

Also, nearby Braddock Bay Park has a hawk-watch platform for bird spotting. During the spring many people volunteer to count the various species flying high over the Rochester skies. Don't forget to bring your binoculars.

Trail Directions
• From the parking area head north across Manitou Beach Road.
• Follow the mulched trail past scrub brush.
• Cross a boardwalk and continue straight on the trail.
• Continue straight (NE) past a trail to the right and a sign "To Hawk Blind BBRR."
• Cross a small wooden bridge.
• Three trails lead from the left into the bird-banding field. Please take the middle one to visit the blind. It has a boardwalk entrance.
• After visiting the blind, return to the main trail and turn left.
• At 0.4 mile reach a "T." Turn right (S).
• The trail bends right and takes you over a series of boardwalks. (The pine woods on the left is a favorite owl resting area.)
• At 0.8 mile, turn left at the trail junction to return to the parking area.

Date Hiked: _____

Notes:

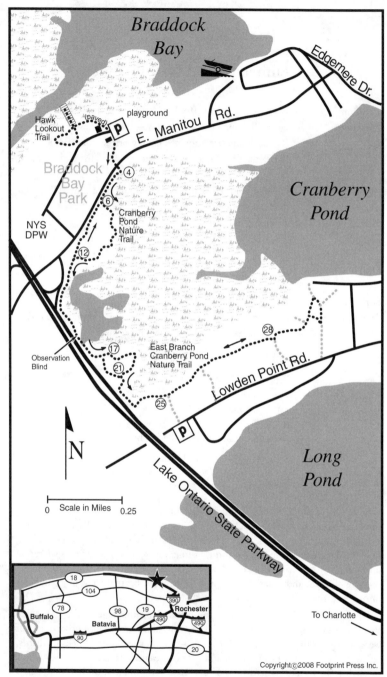

Braddock Bay

Edgemere Dr.

playground

Hawk Lookout Trail

(paved)

E. Manitou Rd.

Cranberry Pond

Braddock Bay Park

④

⑥

Cranberry Pond Nature Trail

NYS DPW

⑫

⑰

Observation Blind

East Branch Cranberry Pond Nature Trail

㉑

㉘

Lowden Point Rd.

㉕

N

Long Pond

0 Scale in Miles 0.25

Lake Ontario State Parkway

18

104

78

98

19

390

Rochester

Buffalo

Batavia

90

490

490

20

To Charlotte

Cranberry Pond Nature Trail

2

Cranberry Pond Nature Trail

Location:	Braddock Bay Park, 199 East Manitou Road, Greece
Directions:	From Lake Ontario State Parkway, take the East Manitou Road exit and head north. Take the first left into Braddock Bay Park. Turn right and follow the road to the parking lot at the end.
Alternate Parking:	Lowden Point Road parking lot. (Look for a white DEC sign that talks about hunting.)
Hiking Time:	2.5 hours full loop
Length:	3.8-miles round trip on Cranberry Pond Nature Trail
	0.6-mile round trip to the Hawk Watch Platform
Difficulty:	
Surface:	Dirt and mulch trail
Trail Markings:	Green trail signs, numbered signs on posts, round blue DEC foot trail markers, square brown hiker markers
Uses:	🚶 Hawk Lookout Trail:
Dogs:	Pets OK on leash
Admission:	Free
Contact:	DEC Region 8
	6274 E. Avon-Lima Road, Avon, NY 14414-9519
	www.dec.ny.gov/outdoor/24428.html
	Town of Greece, Parks Dept.
	1 Vince Tofany Blvd, Greece, NY 14612
	www.greeceny.gov

An extensive cattail marsh, Braddock Bay, and several ponds are the central features of Braddock Bay Park. Located on the east side of Braddock Bay, it has a boat marina, picnic areas, the Cranberry Pond Nature Trail and the famous Hawk Lookout Platform. From the platform, visitors can witness the spectacular spring bird migration featuring hawks, owls and eagles. Some years, over 140,000 birds of prey are observed in migration over the park between February and June, and also in August during southerly winds.

The Cranberry Pond Nature Trail meanders along the edge of the Cranberry Pond wetlands. Several lookouts and a viewing blind allow close observation of waterfowl and other wetland wildlife such as Canada geese, wood ducks, mallards, red wing black birds, great blue herons, hawks, eagles, etc. The trail also winds through a small mature hardwood forest. Trees found here include black cherry, shagbark hickory, and white oak. Number signs on posts provide information about the trees you're passing, as well as descriptions of invasive species, birds that migrate through here, and plant succession. Plan some extra time to read and learn as you walk this trail.

Hawk Lookout Trail Directions (wheelchair accessible)
- From the parking area, north of the lodge, head toward blue sign "Nature Trail Boardwalk - Hawk Lookout."
- The paved trail will arch, turn to gravel, then become boardwalk, before reaching the 6-foot-high viewing platform.

Date Hiked: _____
Notes:

Cranberry Pond Nature Trail Directions
- From the parking area, follow the green sign "Cranberry Pond Nature Trail," passing station numbers 2 & 3.
- Cross East Manitou Road.
- Begin to see the water's edge at station 4.
- Walk south along a mowed grass area, passing several stations.
- At station 6, turn left into the woods on a mulched trail. This trail is marked by round, blue DEC foot-trail markers.
- Continue straight at the next junction. (Left leads to a bench.)
- After station 12, begin to see the road. At the brown sign with a yellow arrow, turn left. (Right will be part of the return loop.)
- Pass station 13, and walk along a grassy area. Watch for muskrat houses sticking out of the cattails.
- Pass station 14. The parkway is to your right.
- At station 15 is the Town of Greece Observation Photographic Blind built by eagle scouts in 2001.
- Continue along the tree line on the grass trail to station 16.
- Bear left to reach station 17 and pass through Aspens. (Left will be the return leg.)
- Pass a bench at station 18, then several more stations.
- After station 21, turn left beside the parkway at the sign "Cranberry Trail East."
- Renter the woods at station 22 and follow the raised path.
- Station 24 has a bench. The paths here are tree lined and marked with square, brown hiker markers.
- After station 25, reach a "T," and turn left. (Right takes you to Lowden Point Road and a parking lot across the street.)
- At station 26, look for the large old tree that was struck by lightening.
- Pass a path to the right (to Lowden Point Road).
- Pass stations 27 and 28. (Across from station 28 is the 3rd side trail to Lowden Point Road.)

Bird watching blind along Cranberry Pond Nature Trail.

• Pass station 29, then a small trail to the left.
• At a "T," turn left. (Right will be part of the return loop). This is a lesser used section of trail.
• At a 3-way junction, continue straight on the main path. (The path to the left goes to a bench. The path to the right goes to houses.)
• Another path to the left leads to houses. You are making the final loop.
• Pass a bench.
• Begin the return leg on Cranberry Trail East, passing the 3 trails on the left that head to Lowden Point Road.
• After station 22, bear left.
• Bear left again at the next junction and pass the observation blind.
• At station 13 enter the woods at the orange flag.
• Follow the mowed grass path and pass station 6.
• At stations 4 & 5, take an immediate left (look carefully, it's hidden in bushes) to cross East Manitou Road and return to the parking lot.

Date Hiked: _____

Notes:

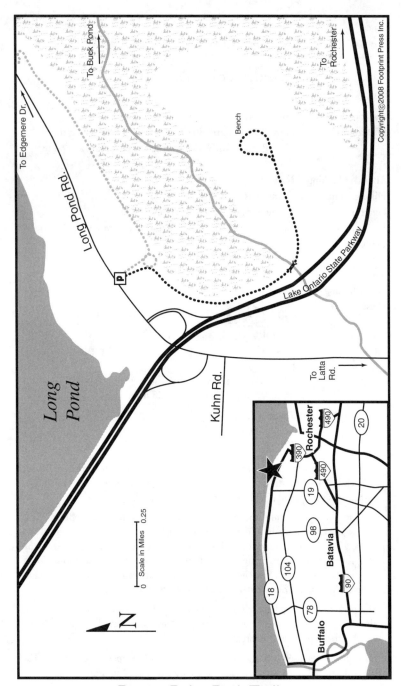

To Edgemere Dr.

To Buck Pond

Long Pond Rd.

To Rochester

Copyright©2008 Footprint Press Inc.

Bench

Lake Ontario State Parkway

P

Long Pond

Kuhn Rd.

To Latta Rd.

Rochester

490

20

390

490

19

98

Batavia

104

90

18

78

Buffalo

0   Scale in Miles   0.25

N

Beatty Point Park Trail

3

Beatty Point Park Trail

Location:	Long Pond Road, Greece
Directions:	From Lake Ontario State Parkway, exit heading north on Long Pond Road. Watch for the gravel parking area to the right.
Alternate Parking:	None
Hiking Time:	75 minutes
Length:	2.5 miles round trip (main, darkened trail)
	1.7 mile round trip (lesser used trail that heads northeast)
Difficulty:	
Surface:	Former hard-packed gravel road
Trail Markings:	None
Uses:	🚶 🚴 🎿 ♿
Dogs:	Pets OK on leash
Admission:	Free
Contact:	DEC Region 8
	6274 E. Avon-Lima Road, Avon, NY 14414-9519
	www.dec.ny.gov/outdoor/24428.html
	Town of Greece, Parks Dept.
	1 Vince Tofany Blvd, Greece, NY 14612
	www.greeceny.gov

Beatty Point is composed primarily of grassy fields on a peninsula that sticks out into Buck Pond. The path is an old road bed that was never developed into a housing tract. It is very popular with bird watchers.

Barn swallows nest under the small bridge over the creek feeding Buck Pond. Marsh wrens are abundant, and an early morning or late evening visit is likely to produce a rail. Both American and least bitterns nest along the edges. After the bridge, there are grasslands being managed for switchgrass. Once the nesting site of many grassland birds, the switchgrass mowing is an attempt to revive the habitat. Stay on the paths to avoid accidentally crushing a bird nest.

The park is also popular with dog owners, and despite the leash requirement, canines are frequently seen running freely around the area. This is probably adversely affecting the bird population.

There is a lesser-used path (also part of the never-developed road system) that runs northeast of the parking area and heads toward Lake Ontario.

Beatty Point Park Trail crosses a wetland creek.

Trail Directions
- From the parking area, pass the double yellow gate with a red stop sign, heading south on the main trail.
- Follow the trail over the bridge.
- Pass the grassland improvement area, marked by a sign about switchgrass.
- At the "Y," choose either direction to loop around the end of the road, then return via the same path.

Date Hiked: _____
Notes:

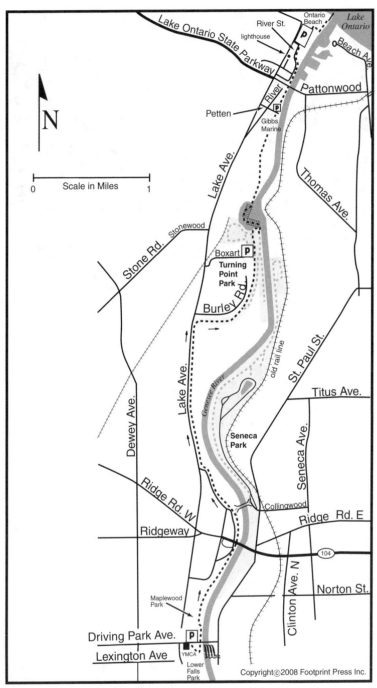

Genesee Riverway Trail

Genesee Riverway Trail

Location:	City of Rochester, from Maplewood Park through Turning Point Park to Lake Ontario
Directions:	Park in the Maplewood Park parking area on Driving Park Avenue, near the Genesee River.
Alternative Parking:	From Lake Avenue in Charlotte, turn east on Boxart Street. The parking area for Turning Point Park is at the end of Boxart Street.
Alternative Parking:	At Ontario Beach Park at the north end of Lake Avenue in Charlotte
Hiking Time:	3 hours one way
Length:	6.5 miles one way
Difficulty:	👣👣
Surface:	Paved path, mowed grass path, dirt path, and sidewalks
Trail Markings:	Large "Genesee River Trail" signs
Uses:	🚶 ⛷ 🚴 (there are some stairs to traverse)
Dogs:	OK on leash
Admission:	Free
Contact:	City of Rochester Bureau of Parks & Recreation 400 Dewey Avenue Rochester, NY 14613 (585) 428-6770

This linear trail is inside the city limits of Rochester and offers good views of the Genesee River from high above, and up close at water level. It begins at the south end of Maplewood Park, passes through Turning Point Park, and ends at Ontario Beach Park on Lake Ontario. Along the way you'll get a view of the Genesee River and Lower Falls, cross under the Driving Park and Memorial Bridges, pass historic King's Landing, and walk the boardwalk over a turning basin in the Genesee River.

History abounds along this area of the gorge. The early settlements of McCrackenville, Carthage, King's Landing, Frankfort, and Castleton are all but memories. Only Charlotte remains a familiar name. With the coming of the Erie Canal, Rochesterville grew. By 1834 the combination of these seven settlements became the city of Rochester.

The parks along this hike are unique public lands. First, manicured Maplewood Park with its rolling hills, perched next to the Genesee River gorge, is home to 14 acres of rose gardens. Next, Turning Point Park covers 100 acres off Lake Avenue at

Boxart Street. This forever-wild park, which sits along the west side of the Genesee River, has docks jutting into the river. A visit will step you back to what Rochester may have looked like 150 years ago. You'll pass old piers where ships tied up. The original docks opened in the 1890s, but only a cement ship comes up the river to deliver its cargo now. This area is the wide-water section of the river where large boats turned around after unloading their cargo. That's how the Turning Point Park got its name. In 1982, a 100-foot long dock was added as a park improvement project. In 2007 the winding pedestrian bridge over Turning Point Basin was added. The end point at Ontario Beach Park offers a beautiful sand beach on the shore of Lake Ontario, a pier that reaches into the lake, and a historic 1905 Dentzel menagerie carousel.

A winter view of Driving Park Bridge from the Genesee River Trail.

Trail Directions
- Begin by walking across Driving Park Avenue toward the YMCA. On the left side of the YMCA parking lot (west side of Driving Park Bridge), pass through the black metal gates where the sign directs you to Lower Falls Park.
- Head down the paved walkway.
- Part way down, take the stairway on the left and double back along the river. (Straight will take you into Lower Falls Park with views of Lower Falls and Middle Falls.) You're rewarded with a great view of Lower Genesee Falls and the Driving Park Bridge.
- At 0.2 mile, pass under Driving Park Bridge.
- Just before heading up a flight of stairs, notice the ruins of an old building ahead near the edge of the gorge. This is the foundation for a refreshment stand built in the early 1900s.

- Climb two flights of stairs to return to Maplewood Park. Be sure to read the historic signs about the underground railroad and the Seneca Indian village. Also directly ahead is a popular winter sledding hill. Children of all ages start at the top next to Lake Avenue and slide toward the Maplewood Park parking lot.
- At 0.3 mile, turn right and follow the fence line as it parallels the river. Genesee River Trail signs will guide you.
- Pass several scenic overlooks with great views of the river gorge.
- Pass under the Veterans Bridge (Route 104) on the paved path.
- Continue following the fence line. Eventually a right turn would take you to a pedestrian bridge over the river to Seneca Park, but that's a separate hike, so continue straight. (See Olmsted/Seneca Trail #58, page 227)
- You'll pass more history: a sign about a palisaded fort of the Indians and a grist stone from Hanford's Mill. Continue along the fence line.
- Pass Eastman Kodak Company's King's Landing Wastewater Treatment plant entrance. Just beyond is a bench with a great view of the river gorge.
- After the bench you'll be walking approximately 1.5 miles on the sidewalk. Turn right on Lake Avenue and continue on the sidewalk.
- Pass the Kodak research laboratories, Holy Sepulchre Cemetery, and Riverside Cemetery.
- After the cemeteries (just before the Charlotte sign), turn right into Turning Point Park.
- Head downhill on a paved path.
- At the first junction continue straight on the paved path. (The trail to the right is part of the Turning Point Park Trail #60, page 235.)
- Pass the Turning Point Park parking lot and another great view of the river below.
- Continue downhill as the trail bends sharply right.
- At river level, turn left and pass through the yellow metal gates, onto the new boardwalk over the turning basin.
- Off the bridge, return to woods. Pass Gibbs Marine.
- Cross Petten Street, then a parking area. Many boats are anchored here.
- Cross under O'Rourke Bridge.
- Pass the old train station.
- Merge onto River Street where you'll pass several restaurants.
- Reach the large City of Rochester/Port of Rochester & Ontario Beach Boat Launch parking lot.
- Continue through the parking lot, past the Port of Rochester building. Then, turn right (E) to the river. Turn left and follow the sidewalk out to the end of the pier.

Date Hiked: _____

Notes:

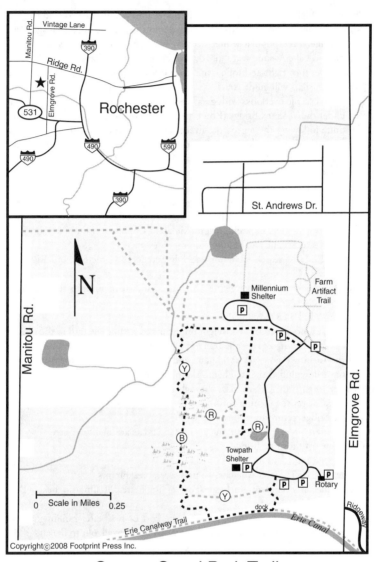

Greece Canal Park Trail

Greece Canal Park Trail

Location:	Greece Canal Park, Greece
Directions:	From Ridge Road West, turn south on Elmgrove Road. Turn west into Greece Canal Park. Take the first left and park immediately on the right.
Alternate Parking:	Towpath Shelter parking area
Hiking Time:	75 minutes
Length:	2.0 mile loop
Difficulty:	🥾 🥾
Surface:	Dirt trail
Trail Markings:	Blue, red and yellow blazes and 4-inch diamond-shaped markers in the same colors
Uses:	🚶
Dogs:	OK on leash
Admission:	Free
Contact:	Monroe County Parks Department 171 Reservoir Avenue, Rochester, NY 14620 www.monroecounty.gov/parks-index.php

This loop takes you through woods and wetlands and includes a 0.2 mile walk along the Erie Canal on the Erie Canalway Trail. This trail can be muddy in wet weather and is suffering from lack of maintenance. Watch for poison ivy along the trail.

Deer Run (blue):	1.4 miles
Canal Trail (red):	0.9 mile
West Trail (orange):	0.4 mile
unnamed trails (grey)	

Trail Directions
- From the parking area head northwest on the trail.
- Quickly reach a "T." Turn right (N).
- The path curves left as another path branches off to the right. Stay on the main path.
- After walking on a short boardwalk, pass another trail branching off to the right.
- Come to a "T." Turn left (S). The remnants of a stone wall are now to your right.
- At 0.3 mile, cross over a stream on a small bridge, then go up a short incline.
- As you approach an opening in the woods, turn left and follow the blue blazes further into the woods.

- Soon red blazes are paired with the blue blazes. Continue following the blazes.
- Arrive at a junction in the trail. Turn right and follow the yellow blazes.
- Cross a series of small boardwalks, continuing to follow the yellow blazes and markers.
- Cross another small bridge.
- Turn right and follow the blue and yellow blazed trail.
- At 0.7 mile turn right on a small trail with blue blazes.
- Carefully watch for the blue blazes as you continue along this narrow trail, as it twists and turns through the woods.
- At 1 mile the trail ends at the edge of a field. Turn left and go up the bank, emerging at the Erie Canal. Turn left and follow the Erie Canalway Trail (E).
- At 1.2 miles, reach the "Greece Canal Park" sign and a dock. Turn left (N) and head downhill on a paved path.
- Pass restrooms, then turn left on a paved path.
- Cross through the Towpath Shelter parking area. Follow the grass area along the main road, heading north.
- Pass a pond on your left.
- Just after the pond, take a left and follow the red blazed path.
- Continue to follow the red blazed trail as it turns left. The dry quarry will now be on your right, with the pond a short distance to your left.
- Take a sharp right turn. You will now be on the blue blazed trail.
- Continue on this trail until 1.9 miles, then bear right and return to parking area.

Date Hiked: _____

Notes:

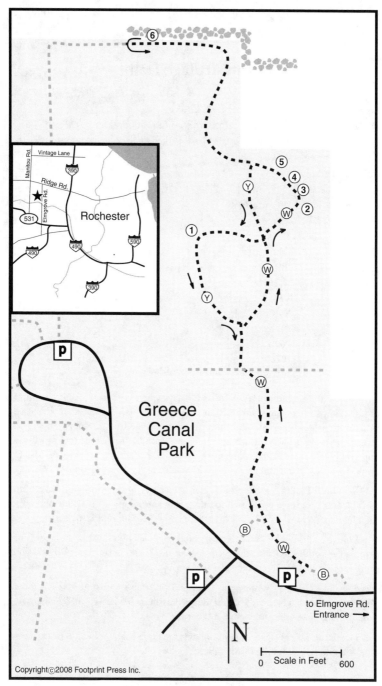

Farm Artifact Trail

Copyright©2008 Footprint Press Inc.

4

Farm Artifact Trail

Location:	Greece Canal Park, Greece
Directions:	From Ridge Road West, turn south on Elmgrove Road. Turn west into Greece Canal Park. The parking area is immediately to your right.
Alternate Parking:	None
Hiking Time:	30 minutes
Length:	1.0 mile loop
Difficulty:	🥾
Surface:	Dirt path
Trail Markings:	Blue, white & yellow blazes
Uses:	🚶
Dogs:	OK on leash
Admission:	Free
Contact:	Monroe County Parks Department 171 Reservoir Avenue, Rochester, NY 14620 www.monroecounty.gov/parks-index.php

As you walk this trail, think back to the days when farmers worked the soil to produce crops. There are stone walls in many places along the way that were used to separate fields. Where do you think the stones came from? Your vision will be assisted by farm artifacts left on the land when farming ceased. This is a treasure hunt trail. The farm artifacts are rusting and disappearing back into the Earth. Look closely and see if you can find what remains of the 6 farm artifacts:

1. Windmill Blades — Windmills catch the energy of the wind and make it do useful work. Windmills were used to pump water, grind grain into flour, and even run sawmills. What do you think the farmer used this windmill for?

2. Plow — This double-bottom plow could be pulled by a horse or a tractor. The two blades would each turn the earth to one side, making furrows. Why do you think each wheel is on a separate axle?

3. Drag — The drag loosens the earth and pulls up small stones. (Remember those stone walls?) The handle could adjust how deep the curved piece would go. Would a farmer use the drag before or after the plow?

4. Hay Rake — This rakes hay into piles for making bales. Some pieces are missing. What do you think the missing pieces looked like?

5. Wagon — The wooden parts of this wagon rotted away. The metal axis and curved parts for steering were left. How long do you think it would take for the wooden parts to rot?

6. Wheel — Envision a bumpy ride in the hay wagon on this metal wheel.

Windmill blades.
One of several artifacts found along the Farm Artifact Trail.

You will be following the blue and white-blazed trail north and use the yellow-blazed side loops on your return journey. Beware of poison ivy along the edges of the trail. This trail suffers from lack of maintenance. You may encounter high weeds and grasses and may have to hunt to find the remaining artifacts.

Trail Directions
- From the parking area head into the woods on a dirt path (N) following the blue blazes.
- Pass a small blue-blazed loop to the left. Stay on the main trail as it winds through the woods.
- At 0.1 mile, the trail will be lined with faint white blazes.
- Continue straight, crossing a wide, semi-maintained path.
- Cross another (mowed) path at 0.2 mile, and continue straight. Notice the stone wall to your left.
- At "Y," bear right. Quickly come to another "Y" and bear right again.
- Immediately bear right. A side path to the left heads to private land.
- The path bears left at a stone wall. Follow the path, with the wall to your right. Watch for artifacts 2, 3, 4, and 5 as you walk beside the wall.
- Pass a yellow-blazed trail on the left. Continue following the white blazes.
- At next intersection, turn left. The stone wall will continue to be on your right.
- At 0.4 mile, turn right and cross the wall where there is a break in the stone.
- Take a sharp right and follow the path. There will be pine trees on your right and deciduous trees on your left.
- At a "T," turn right. (Left leads to a field.)
- Recross the stone wall and immediately turn right at the "T." Continue straight and head back into the woods. Be very careful, as this part of the trail is not well maintained.
- Cross the stone wall one final time, then turn left. The wall will now be on your left.
- Bear right at the"Y."
- Bear right at a 2nd "Y."
- Cross both mowed paths that you crossed earlier in the hike. Continue to retrace your steps on the blue-blazed trail until you emerge from the woods at the parking area.

Date Hiked: _____

Notes:

Northampton Park

This 973 acre park is unique because of the active "working" farm within its boundaries. Originally, when the park was dedicated in 1964, it was named Salmon Creek Park. But, Northampton was later selected to honor the area's rich history and the former Township of Northampton.

The park, which straddles the Sweden-Ogden town line, combines a downhill ski slope and rope tow, a model airplane field, Salmon Creek, the Pulver House of the Ogden Historical Society, and Springdale Farm — a demonstration farm with chickens, peacocks, turkeys, horses, cows, goats, bunnies, pigs, lambs, and bulls. It's a great place to explore with children either before or after a hike. The farm is open Monday through Saturday from 10 AM to 4 PM and Sundays, noon to 4 PM.

Geese paddle along on the Springdale Farm pond.

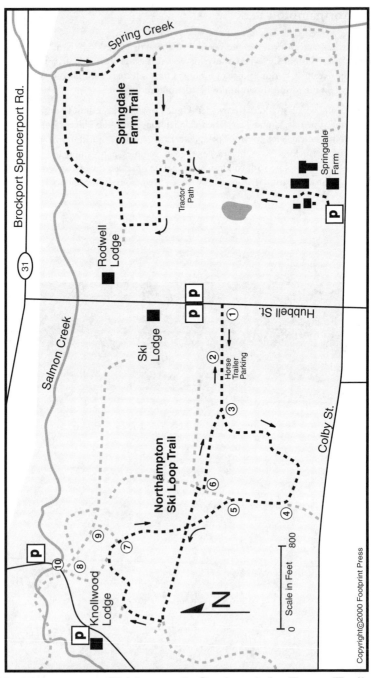

Northampton Ski Loop & Springdale Farm Trails

Springdale Farm Trail

Location:	Northampton Park, Colby Street, Ogden
Directions:	Take Route 31 west from Rochester. Turn south on Route 36 then west on Colby Street. Park in the Springdale Farm parking area.

Alternative Parking: None
Hiking Time: 45 minutes
Length: 1.7 mile loop
Difficulty:

Surface:	Gravel, mulch, dirt, and mowed-grass paths
Trail Markings:	None
Uses:	🚶 🎿 🐎
Dogs:	OK on leash
Admission:	Free
Contact:	Monroe County Parks Department
	171 Reservoir Avenue
	Rochester, NY 14620
	(585 256-4950
	Springdale Farm
	operated by Heritage Christian Home, Inc.
	(585) 352-5320

On this easy-to-walk loop you'll pass the barns and animal pens of Springdale Farm, then pass a pond which is home to geese and ducks. A swing, picnic tables and benches make this a restful place to stop before or after your hike. The trail then leads through a forest, skirts the edge of a farm field and enters another forest. You'll walk high on a ledge overlooking Spring Creek, then follow the edge of farm fields back to the pond and barn area.

Trail Directions
- From the parking area follow the paved path past Springdale Farms barn area.
- The gravel road leads from behind the barns and past a pond.
- At the "Woodlot Trail" sign, the trail turns to mulch and enters the woods.
- Bear left (NE) at the big red sign and follow the mulched path through a beech tree forest.
- Pass two trails to the right. (They lead to a classroom area and loop back to the big red sign.)
- At 0.4 mile, emerge to a farm field. Turn left (W) and follow the edge of the field.
- Pass a grass trail on the left.

- At the bottom of the sled hill (before heading uphill) turn right (N) and cross the edge of the field.
- Bear right again (E) and follow along the edge of the woods. You're now on the opposite side of the field from where you started.
- At 0.6 mile, enter the woods.
- At 0.9 mile, climb a small hill. Spring Creek is in a gully to your left as you walk through a mature pine forest.
- Pass through a shrub field.
- At 1.1 miles, reach a junction and turn right (W). (Left is a loop that leads toward Colby Street.)
- Follow the edge of a farm field. The trail bends several times. Keep the farm fields to your left.
- Pass a small mowed path to the left. (This leads toward Colby Street and loops back around the farm fields.)
- At 1.4 miles, meet the gravel path. Turn left (SW) and head toward the barns and parking area.

Date Hiked: _____

Notes:

Northampton Ski Loop Trail

Location:	Northampton Park, Hubbell Street, Ogden
Directions:	Take Route 31 west from Rochester. After passing Route 36, turn south on Hubbell Street. Park on the west side of Hubbell Street in the southernmost section of the Ski Lodge parking area.
Alternative Parking:	On the east side of Hubbell Street
Hiking Time:	1 hour
Length:	2.0 mile loop (see the map on page 40)
Difficulty:	👣
Surface:	Mowed-grass path
Trail Markings:	Blue-and-white metal signs on wooden posts at some trail junctions
Uses:	🚶 ⛷ 🏇
Dogs:	OK on leash
Admission:	Free
Contact:	Monroe County Parks Department 171 Reservoir Avenue Rochester, NY 14620 (585) 256-4950

The vegetation along the trail is mostly tall bushes and young trees. It's the perfect habitat for birds. While hiking, you'll be serenaded by the honk of pheasants and the trill of songbirds. In late summer you can pick berries from bushes along the 10-foot wide, mowed-grass trail. In winter, glide easily along on skis.

Trail Directions

- Leave the parking area from the corner farthest from the ski lodge, heading southwest through a grove of young pines.
- Cross the grass to to a sign "Horse Trailer Parking" and junction marker #2.
- Continue straight (W) on the mowed-grass path.
- Turn left (S) at junction marker #3.
- The path goes between woods and a field. At 0.5 mile, reach junction marker #4 and turn right (N).
- Notice the old stone wall inside the woods along the right side of the trail — a sure sign that this was once farm land. Farmers cleared stones from their fields and piled them along property lines.
- At junction marker #5 bear left (N).

- After the wide mowed area, turn left. You're now heading west.
- When the path curves at 0.9 mile, bear right. (Two paths lead off to the left.)
- The path is gravel covered for a short stretch.
- Bear right again past a trail to the left. You're now heading east.
- The trail bends several times.
- At 1.2 miles bear right (E), passing a trail to the left.
- At junction marker #7 turn right (S).
- At the wide mowed-grass area turn left (E).
- Reach an intersection at 1.5 miles and turn right (S).
- Quickly reach junction marker #6 and turn left (S).
- Cross a short gravel stretch, then the trail turns to dirt as you walk through the woods.
- At 1.7 miles, turn left (E) at junction marker #3, and return to the parking area.

Date Hiked: _____

Notes:

James Miles and Michael Peter enjoy bird watching as they hike.

Southwest
Section

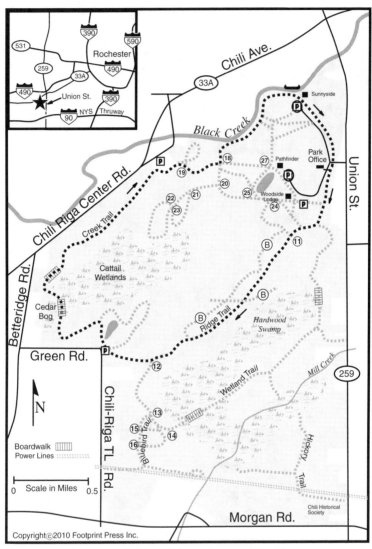

Creek & Ridge Loop Trail

9

Creek & Ridge Loop Trail

Location:	Black Creek Park, Union Street, Chili
Directions:	Take the Union Street exit off Interstate 490 and head south on Union Street. Turn right to enter Black Creek Park and follow the park road left to the parking area near Woodside Lodge.
Alternative Parking:	At the north end of the park road near Sunnyside Lodge.
Hiking Time:	2 hours and 15 minutes
Length:	4.2 mile loop
Difficulty:	👣 👣 👣 👣
Surface:	Mowed-grass and dirt paths
Trail Markings:	Some junctions are marked with blue-and-white numbered signs on wooden posts
Uses:	🥾 🎿 🐎
Dogs:	OK on leash
Admission:	Free
Contact:	Monroe County Parks Department 171 Reservoir Avenue, Rochester, NY 14620 (585) 256-4950 www.monroecounty.gov/parks-index.php

Black Creek is the centerpiece of this park in southwestern Monroe County. Purchased in 1963, the park has large tracts of undeveloped, rolling hills with two small ponds. Its trails wind through tall brush and young forest areas which attract many kinds of birds. Six-foot wide paths are mowed throughout the park creating many possible hiking or cross-country skiing loops. Deer are plentiful in the park.

Trail Directions
- From the southeast corner of the parking area, walk east along the mulched trail.
- Turn right (S) and pass a gate.
- Turn right at the "T."
- At 0.2 mile, pass benches on the right overlooking a depression area.
- Pass junction marker #11 and a small trail into the woods on the right. Continue straight (SW).
- At 1.0 mile, enter the woods. Bear left to stay on the main trail.
- Stay on the main trail, passing a small trail to the right.
- Reach junction marker #12 at 1.2 miles. Continue straight (W).
- Cross a wooden bridge.

- Bear right toward the red barn.
- At 1.5 miles cross the parking area.
- Bear left around the far side of the pond.
- Half way down the pond, turn left (W) and head uphill into the woods.
- Follow the top of an open ridge then descend into woods.
- At 2.1 miles, cross a small boardwalk then proceed through a wet area.
- Cross a makeshift bridge then a small boardwalk over a creek.
- Reach a mowed area.
- Reach a "T" at 2.3 miles. Turn right (NE). (Left leads to a road.)
- Bear right staying on the wide path when a small trail heads left.
- At 3.1 miles, reach a "T." Turn right (S). (Left leads to Chili Riga Center Road.)
- Continue straight past a trail to the left.
- Turn right to cross a small wooden bridge to junction marker #19.
- At junction marker #18 turn left (NE).
- The trail bends right and Black Creek gully comes into view on the left.
- Pass a trail to the right.
- Reach junction marker #17 with another trail to the right at 3.5 miles.
- Walk through a grassy picnic area.
- At the end of the mowed area, follow the gravel trail uphill.
- Continue straight.
- At 3.7 miles, just before the park road, turn left (SE) on a grass path.
- At 3.9 miles reach a park road. Turn left along the road, then bear left (SE) onto the grass path.
- Continue straight across a park road.
- Follow the grass path back to the parking area.

Date Hiked: _____

Notes:

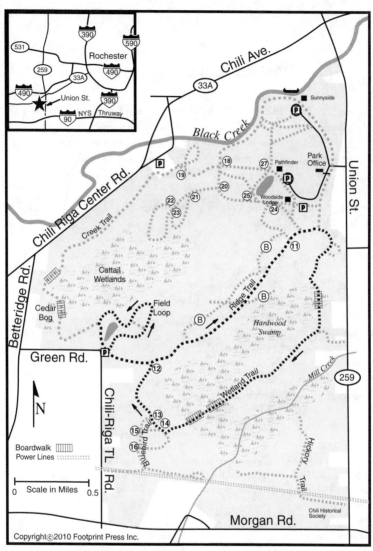

Wetland & Ridge Loop Trail and
Black Creek Field Loop Trail

10

Wetland & Ridge Loop Trail

Location:	Black Creek Park, Chili-Riga Town Line Road, Chili
Directions:	Take the Union Street exit off Interstate 490 and head south on Union Street. Turn west on Morgan Road, then north on Chili-Riga Town Line Road. The parking area is at the corner of Green Road and Chili-Riga Town Line Road
Alternative Parking:	Parking areas off Union Street
Hiking Time:	2 hours
Length:	4-mile loop
Difficulty:	👞👞 👞👞
Surface:	Mowed-grass path
Trail Markings:	Junctions are marked with blue-and-white numbered signs on wooden posts
Uses:	🚶 🎿 🐎
Dogs:	OK on leash
Admission:	Free
Contact:	Monroe County Parks Department 171 Reservoir Avenue, Rochester, NY 14620 (585) 256-4950 www.monroecounty.gov/parks-index.php

This trail is found in the less-used section of Black Creek Park. The wide mowed paths are perfect for a quiet stroll to enjoy sunshine and the sounds of nature. Much of the trail passes through scrub brush fields, which a variety of birds call home.

Trail Directions
- From the parking area, bear right (S) past the red barn. At the wide grassy area (horse trailer parking) turn left to find the beginning of the trail. Look for a 3' post with a white arrow.
- Cross the bridge over a small creek.
- At 0.2 mile, reach junction marker #12. Continue straight on the Ridge Trail. Pass a blue trail to the left.
- Pass a picnic table
- Pass a blue trail intersection. Continue straight.
- Continue straight past junction #11.
- Pass a view into a field on your left.

50

- Bear right at the next junction. (Left leads to the main park shelter area).
- Bear right at the next two junctions.
- Pass a bench.
- Enter a pine forest.
- Cross a floating boardwalk as you head into Hardwood Swamp.
- Pass a trail to the left.
- Pass underneath an apple tree next to old farm machinery. (Note: This land was former farmland. Notice all the rock walls denoting the edge of an old field.)
- Pass a bench facing a field.
- Pass a bench facing the wetlands.
- Cross another floating boardwalk
- Turn right at the "T".
- At junction #14 turn right passing a McCormick Deering #7 farm machinery.
- Bear right through junction #13.
- Turn left at junction #12 to return to the parking lot.

Date Hiked: _____

Notes:

11

Black Creek Field Loop Trail

Location:	Black Creek Park, Chili-Riga Town Line Road, Chili
Directions:	Take the Union Street exit off Interstate 490 and head south on Union Street. Turn west on Morgan Road, then north on Chili-Riga Town Line Road. The parking area is at the corner of Green Road and Chili-Riga Town Line Road
Alternative Parking:	None
Hiking Time:	25 minutes
Length:	0.8 mile loop
Difficulty:	
Surface:	Mowed-grass path
Trail Markings:	None
Uses:	

Dogs:	OK on leash
Admission:	Free
Contact:	Monroe County Parks Department
	171 Reservoir Avenue, Rochester, NY 14620
	(585) 256-4950
	www.monroecounty.gov/parks-index.php

If you would like a quick introduction to Black Creek Park, try this easy loop around a field and pond on a wide mowed-grass path.

Trail Directions
• From the parking area, pass on the left side of the red barn heading toward the old tan cement block restrooms.
• Turn left and follow the woods edge. The forest is on your right and mowed grass is to your left.
• The mowed area takes you around the perimeter of the field, always with the woods to your right.
• Pass a cutoff mowed path on your left.
• At 0.6 mile the pond will come into view. Bear right (NW) and cross the grass covered dike.
• Bear right to keep the pond on your left while entering the next field.
• Pass the Creek Trail entrance into the woods.
• At the south end of the pond, walk to the parking area.

Date Hiked: _____

Notes:

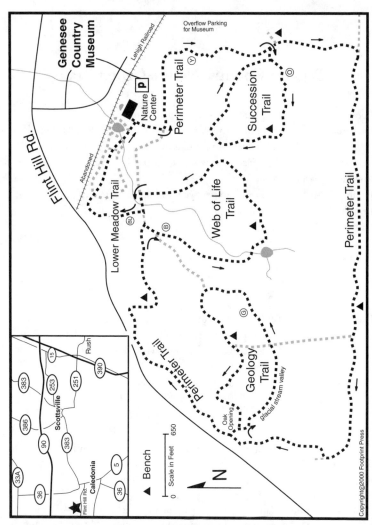

Genesee Country Nature Center Trails

12

Genesee Country Nature Center Trails

Location:	Genesee Country Museum, Mumford
Directions:	From Route 36, turn west onto Flint Hill Road just north of Caledonia. Turn left into Genesee Country Museum and follow the signs to the nature center parking area.
Alternative Parking:	None
Hiking Time:	2 hours (or more if you read the interpretive signs)
Length:	3.5 mile loop
Difficulty:	🥾 🥾 🥾 🥾
Surface:	Mowed-grass, mulched, and dirt paths
Trail Markings:	Wooden trail signs at junctions
Uses:	🚶 🎿
Dogs:	Pets are NOT allowed
Admission:	Adults $2.50, Seniors $2.00, Children 4-16 $1.50, Children under 4 free. Free with admission to Genesee Country Museum
Contact:	Genesee Country Nature Center Flint Hill Road, Mumford, NY 14511 (585) 538-6822 www.gcv.org

Genesee Country Museum is a reconstructed community from the 1800s with 57 restored and fully furnished buildings. Stroll the streets and visit each shop, home, school, and church as costumed villagers demonstrate life from a bygone century.

Genesee Country Nature Center is part of Genesee Country Museum. The nature center has a classroom building with nature exhibits, a lily pond, a butterfly garden, and nearly five miles of hiking and cross-country skiing trails. Special events such as guided hikes, birds of prey day, nesting bird surveys, and programs on area wildlife and history are held throughout the year.

Admission to the museum includes admission to the nature center. Or, you can purchase nature center admission separately. In the summer the nature center is open Tuesday - Friday 10 AM to 4 PM, and Saturday - Sunday, 10 AM to 5 PM. It is closed Mondays. Call (585) 538-6822 for up to date information on admission fees and hours of operation.

The trails within Genesee Country Nature Center are mostly flat with a few rolling hills. The land was once farmed and now contains a mixture of fields and young forest. We particularly enjoyed the interpretive signs along these trails. On the Succession Trail, they teach the process of succession from farm field back to forest. Trees are labeled on the Perimeter Trail. A vernal (or seasonal) pond is the highlight of the Web of Life Trail. It's the breeding site of spotted and blue-spotted salamanders.

The Geology Trail teaches the unique geology of this area, pointing out ancient waterfalls from glacial streams, marine fossils, and oak openings. Approximately 4,000 years ago a major drought caused the demise of many native species of trees and allowed midwestern prairie plants to move east. It created fields of tall grass prairies surrounded by oak forests — an oak opening. The Indians noticed that these grass openings were havens from bugs and allowed them to get a broader view of approaching enemies so they kept the grasslands open with fire. The absence of trees in the oak openings made them easy targets for farmers. As white settlers moved in, many of the oak openings were put to use to raise crops.

This oak opening is one of fewer than 20 oak openings remaining in the world. It was spared because limestone is only a few inches below the surface so it was hard to plow and virtually impossible to sink fence posts. The other area oak opening can be found at Quinn Oak Openings in Rush. (see trail #15, page 65.)

Interpretive signs like this one identifying an old stone wall, help the walker learn about geology and history along the nature trails.

The loop described here samples each of the trails, giving you a broad look at this special landscape. There are many opportunities to shorten your hike. If you want to do a shorter hike, the loop distances from the nature center are as follows:

Perimeter Trail (yellow)	1.9 miles
Geology Trail (green)	1.8 miles
Succession Trail (orange)	1.1 miles
Web of Life Trail (blue)	0.8 mile
Lower Meadow Trail (black)	0.3 mile

The nature center personnel told us that the Web of Life Trail was the most heavily used. We could see that by its well worn path. But, by far, our favorite trail was the Geology Trail because of its unusual geologic characteristics and the excellent signs along the way that helped us understand the land we stood upon.

Trail Directions
• Head out the back door of the nature center building.
• Bear left (S) on the yellow Perimeter Trail.
• Turn left (S) at the "T" to stay on the Perimeter Trail.
• At 0.3 mile, turn right onto the orange Succession Trail.
• Follow the orange arrow, bearing left.
• Reach a junction at 0.8 mile and turn left.
• Quickly reach a "T," and turn right (SE) to return to the Perimeter Trail.
• Bear right. (Left leads to a parking area.)
• At 0.9 mile the trail bends right so you're now walking west in a young forest.
• Reach a bent tree at 1.3 miles and a bench shortly thereafter.
• At 1.4 miles, pass an unmarked trail to the right. Continue straight.
• The trail bends right and begins heading north.
• The trail bends right again. (The trail straight ahead is blocked off.)
• At 1.6 miles, reach a ridge. The trail bends left (NW) to follow the ridge then does a U turn to descend the ridge.
• Turn right (S) at 1.7 miles onto the green Geology Trail.
• Soon bear right (S) to head into the glacial stream valley.
• Pass an extinct waterfall then proceed through a valley formed by glacial floods 14,000 years ago.
• At 1.9 miles, pass an intersection. Continue straight.
• Pass remains of a high stone wall at 2.0 miles.
• Reach a "T," and turn left (W) onto the Geology Trail.
• Pass a bench at 2.1 miles as you walk a ridge.
• Follow the arrow sign, bearing right.
• Head downhill then pass over another old stone wall.
• At 2.3 miles, cross a small wooden bridge.
• Enter the oak savannah (also called an oak opening).
• Continue straight past a trail to the left.
• Reach a "T." Turn right (E).
• At 2.4 miles pass an old well on your right.
• Pass a bench at 2.6 miles, then pass through another old stone wall.
• At 2.8 miles turn right (SW) at the "T" onto the blue Web of Life Trail.
• Bear left.

- Cross a stream culvert. Vernal Pond is to your right.
- Pass a bench at 3.0 miles.
- Head downhill.
- Turn left (W) at the "T" onto The Perimeter Trail.
- Quickly take a right (N) onto The Lower Meadow Trail.
- At 3.4 miles, emerge to the meadow.
- Continue straight passing a series of mowed paths in the meadow to return to the nature center building.

Date Hiked: _____

Notes:

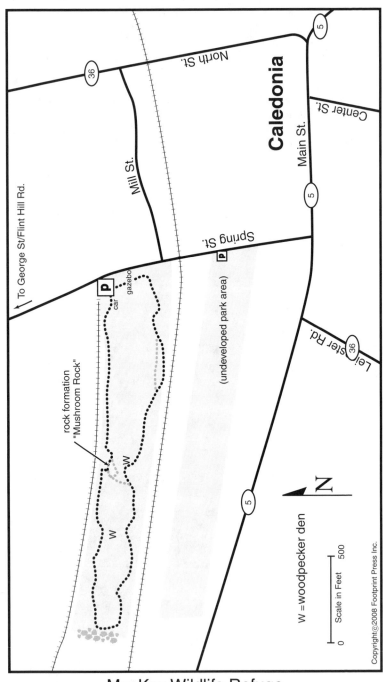

MacKay Wildlife Refuge

To George St/Flint Hill Rd.

36

North St.

Mill St.

Caledonia

Main St.

Center St.

5

5

Spring St.

P

P

(undeveloped park area)

Leister Rd.

36

5

rock formation
"Mushroom Rock"

gazebo

car

W

W

W

N

W = woodpecker den

Scale in Feet

0   500

Copyright©2008 Footprint Press Inc.

58

13

MacKay Wildlife Refuge

Location:	Spring Street, Caledonia
Directions:	At the monument in Caledonia (junction of Routes 5 and 36) head west on Route 5. Take the first right onto Spring Street (almost across from the Giggling Pig). Go 0.2 mile, over railroad tracks, and pass Mill Street. The refuge will be on the left. Watch for a green "MacKay Wildlife Refuge" sign. (Pass the first refuge sign for the undeveloped area before the railroad tracks, at 0.1 mile)

Alternative Parking: None

Hiking Time:	1 hour (includes taking time to read the signs)
Length:	0.9 mile loop
Difficulty:	🥾 (a few short stairs)
Surface:	Mulch
Trail Markings:	None
Uses:	🚶
Dogs:	OK on leash
Admission:	Free
Contact:	Village of Caledonia
	3095 Main St, Caledonia, NY 14423
	(585) 538-4150

Land for this refuge was donated to the Village of Caledonia in 1973 by Mrs. Marianna MacKay Wilkins. It's comprised of two parcels, an undeveloped area of about 10 acres, plus 16 acres with the trail you'll hike. Through volunteer efforts, development began in 2004.

What they've developed is a real treasure, especially if you like learning about geology, nature, or history. Signs abound along this pleasant woods walk, explaining the natural and man-made sights along the way. Trees are labeled, short side trails lead to woodpecker dens (trees full of woodpecker holes), and the trail is dotted with bluebird houses and benches. You'll see and learn about rocks containing fossils, moss covered fieldstone, chert, water lyme, karsts and more. Don't worry if you're not familiar with these rocks and formations - helpful signs will explain it all - that's why the time estimate has built-in time for reading signs. You can walk this trail quickly, but at least the first time, plan to take your time.

Rich Freeman points to a woodpecker den.

Trail Directions
- From the parking lot, walk straight (W) on the trail, passing the remains of the MacKay car. (It's a 1950 Pontiac Silverstreak without an engine.)
- The loop trail is obvious and easy to follow. (See the map for a cut-off trail midway along the loop, in case you need to shorten the distance.)

Date Hiked: _____

Notes:

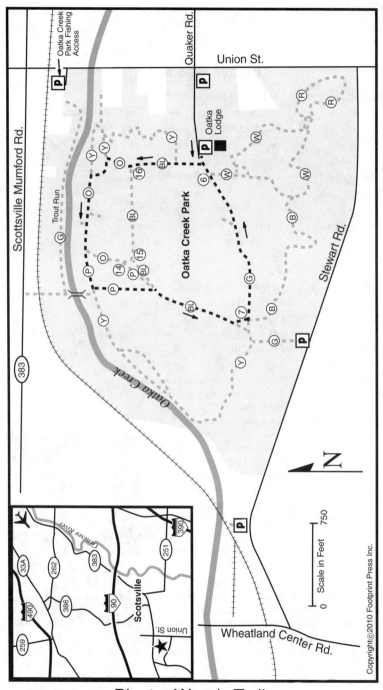

Plaster Woods Trail

14

Plaster Woods Trail

Location:	Oatka Creek Park, Scottsville
Directions:	From Scottsville, head west on Route 383 (Scottsville Mumford Road.) Turn south on Union Street and west into the parking area of Oatka Creek Park at the end of Quaker Road.

Alternative Parking: The parking area south of the railroad tracks on Union Street

The pull-off area on Stewart Road

Hiking Time:	1 hour
Length:	2.0 mile loop
Difficulty:	👢👢
Surface:	Gravel, mowed-grass, and dirt paths
Trail Markings:	Colored blazes on trees, some numbered posts
Uses:	🚶 🎿
Dogs:	OK on leash
Admission:	Free
Contact:	Monroe County Parks Department 171 Reservoir Avenue, Rochester, NY 14620 (585) 256-4950 www.monroecounty.gov/parks-index.php

Under this lush, wooded park lies a soft-gray colored rock called gypsum. Gypsum was used by early farmers as fertilizer, later becoming this country's first cement. Today it is used in wallboard for home construction. Chemically, gypsum is calcium sulfate and gradually turns soil sour (or acidic). Because dogwood, azalea, and mosses prefer this type of soil, these types of vegetation abound in Oatka Creek Park.

When the trail nears the south side of Oatka Creek, you will notice many pits and mounds, remnants of where workers dug gypsum by hand over 150 years ago. They hauled it to the surface with ropes, loaded it into small carts, and pulled it by mules to a mill nearby. You may also find old grist mill foundations and signs of an early settler's log cabin. To fully

Marcy Fenton,
Alex James Clar, and
dalmations TJ and Dooley
stretch their legs on Plaster
Woods Trail.

Fly fishing in Oatka Creek.

explore the gypsum pits and mounds, wander the trails in the northeast part of the
park, south of Oatka Creek.

Oatka Creek Park is best known for brown trout fishing in Oatka Creek. You're
likely to see people fly fishing in the creek. And, if you enjoy bird watching, this is
the place. Watch for downy woodpeckers, flickers, eastern bluebirds and many others, especially in the scrub brush fields.

Trails within Oatka Park:

Color	Name	Distance
Black	Black Billed Cuckoo	0.93 mile
Blue	Bluebird	0.56 mile
Orange	Gypsum Hollow	0.5 mile
Red	Maple Hill	0.5 mile
Green	Old Burrell Road	0.9 mile
Green	Trout Run	0.77 mile
Purple	Warbler Loop	0.52 mile
White	White Trail	0.91 mile
Yellow	Woodland	0.82 mile

Trail Directions
• From the parking area, head west on the old gravel road, passing Oatka Lodge on
  the left.
• Turn right (N) just past the yellow guardrail, onto a dirt trail.
• Pass the Yellow trail to the right.
• Continue straight, as you pass the black trail on the left.
• At 0.6 mile, the trail reaches a "T." Turn left following the orange trail.
• The trail "T's" again. Turn left continuing to follow orange.
• You'll begin to see potholes on both your left and right.
• Pass a trail first to the left, then one to the right.
• Continue straight, now on the purple trail. (The orange trail turns left.) Oatka
  Creek is now on your right.

- At the next intersection, turn left following the purple trail. (Straight becomes a yellow trail. To the right is a green trail leading to an old cement bridge over Oatka Creek with good views of the creek.)
- Black and purple trails enter from the left. Turn right onto the black trail.
- Bear left at the "Y."
- Come to a 4-way intersection. Turn left (E) onto a gravel, green blazed trail.
- Pass an unmarked side trail to the left.
- Pass the white trail entering from the right. Proceed past the gate, back to your car.

Bonus:

If you would like to see more of this park and up-close views of Oatka Creek, drive north on Union Street. After crossing the creek look left, and park in the Oatka Creek Park Fishing Access lot. Follow the path from the southwest corner to the creek. You are able to walk along the creek (following green-blazed Trout Run) to the concrete bridge (at 0.7 mile) before having to turn around. Walking this additional section takes about 45 minutes.

Date Hiked: _____

Notes:

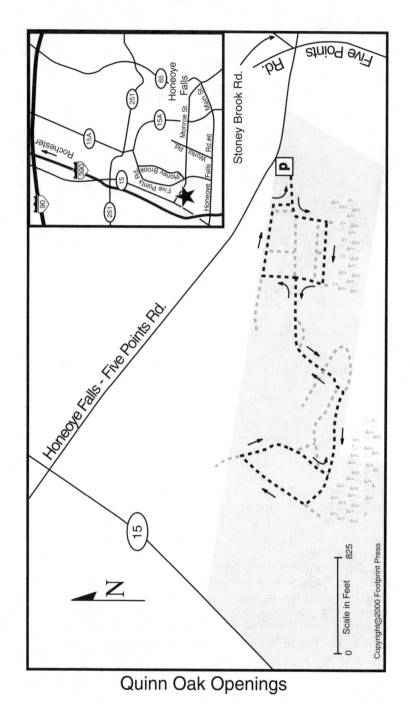

Quinn Oak Openings

15

Quinn Oak Openings

Location:	Honeoye Falls-Five Points Road, Rush
Directions:	From Route 15 (south of Rochester), turn east on Honeoye Falls-Five Points Road. Watch for the Quinn Oak Openings parking area on the south side of Honeoye Falls-Five Points Road.
Additional Parking:	None
Hiking Time:	45 minutes
Length:	1.5 mile loop
Difficulty:	
Surface:	Dirt and mowed field trails
Trail Markings:	None
Uses:	🚶 🎿
Dogs:	OK
Admission:	Free
Contact:	N.Y.S. Department of Environmental Conservation – Forestry 7291 Coon Road, Bath, NY 14810 (607) 776-2165 ext. 10 www.dec.state.ny.us

The sign at the parking area reads "Quinn Oak Openings – Area of Exceptional Forest Character." We'll vouch for the exceptional character of the forests, grass fields, scrub brush fields, and swamps. This wonderfully diverse area is home to many birds, butterflies, animals, and over 400 species of plants. It's also a magical place for humans to wander.

Approximately 4,000 years ago a major drought caused the demise of many native species of trees and allowed midwestern prairie plants to move east. It created fields of tall grass prairies surrounded by oak forests – an oak opening. The Indians noticed that these grass openings were havens from bugs and allowed them to get a broader view of approaching enemies so they kept the grasslands open with fire. The absence of trees in the oak openings made them easy targets for farmers. As white settlers moved in, many of the oak openings were put to use to raise crops.

Quinn Oak Openings is one of fewer than 20 oak openings remaining in the world. Like another opening close by (see the Genesee Country Nature Center Trails on page 53), it was spared because limestone is only a few inches below the surface. This land was privately owned and was used to graze cows. The farmers continued periodic burnings to encourage grass growth. Today, D.E.C. continues this practice to save this unique resource.

The trails can be a challenge to follow. They may be overgrown if it's been awhile since the last mowing or obscured by a blanket of leaves in fall. Sometimes the D.E.C. mows new channels through the grasslands, so the trails shown on the map may vary. Even so, this area is worth exploration. It's unlikely that you'll run into other humans. You're much more likely to scare up deer during your walk. Pay attention to the trees along the way. You'll find rare cinquapin oak and prickly ash. The grass is called Indian grass and grows 6 to 7 feet tall. It's quite a sight in September at its full height with seed heads waving in the autumn breeze.

Trail Directions
- Pass the blue metal gate as you head west on a wide, mowed-grass path. (You're not likely to notice the trails on the right.)
- Turn left (S) onto the first trail to the left. It will appear as a clearing comes into view.
- Take the second right (W) onto a 20-foot wide, uneven weedy swath. (Heading straight past this turnoff will land you in a swamp.)
- Pass a mowed trail to the right.
- Turn right at the "T," passing mowed strips.
- Cross a mowed-grass area, then turn left (W) onto the main trail at 0.3 mile.
- At the "Y" you have a choice. Go left for high, dry ground or, bear right for level, potentially wet ground. The paths converge in 100 feet.
- Stay on the main trail (two tire tracks) as it bends left.
- Pass an intersecting trail and cross a seasonal creek swale. Continue straight on the main path.
- Enter a young forest. (A small trail enters from the right, but we bet you won't see it.)
- At 0.4 mile, turn right (W) at the "T" junction.
- Continue straight past a trail to the right. (This will be part of the return loop.)
- The trail will become rocky and hilly.
- Turn right (N) at the "T" junction.
- The trail bed returns to dirt and mowed grass.
- Turn right (SW) at the "T" junction to stay on the wide mowed path. (The path to the left dead-ends.)
- Bear right and pass a small trail to the left. (You can walk the small trail loops as shown on the map but they may not be maintained.)
- Pass a second small trail on the left.
- At 0.9 mile, turn left (E) at the "T" junction.
- At the next junction, turn left (NE). (The path bearing right loops through a 0.1-mile swampy area and should only be taken if the trails are dry.)
- Immediately pass a small, barely visible trail on your left.
- Continue past the seasonal stream and another trail junction. (This is where the 0.1-mile swampy loop returns.)

- At the "Y" junction, choose either option. A right will take you over high ground, left will be low ground. The paths converge in a short distance.
- At 1.2 miles, turn left (N) when you see a wide mowed area to your right.
- Turn right (E) at the "T" junction. (The trail to the left meanders through moss-covered rocks in a forest, but dead-ends.)
- Pass several small trails to the right.
- The trail will bend sharply right (S) and meet the main trail.
- Turn left (E) onto the main trail for a short distance back to the parking area.

Date Hiked: _____

Notes:

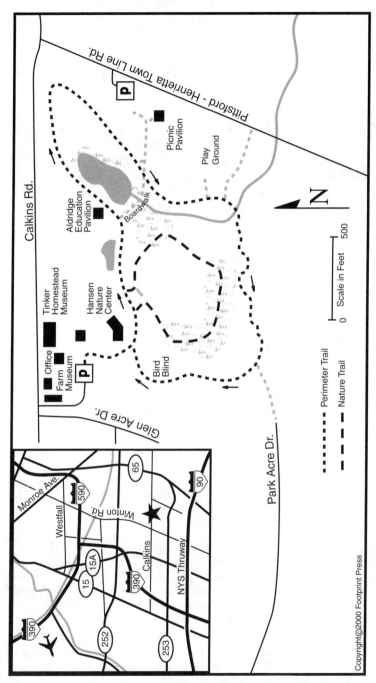

Tinker Nature Park Trails

Pitsford - Henrietta Town Line Rd.

Calkins Rd.

P

Picnic Pavilion

Play Ground

N

Scale in Feet
0   500

Aldridge Education Pavilion

Boardwalk

Tinker Homestead Museum

Hansen Nature Center

Office

Farm Museum

P

Bird Blind

Glen Acre Dr.

Park Acre Dr.

····· Perimeter Trail
– – – Nature Trail

Monroe Ave.

Westfall

590

65

Winton Rd.

90

15A

15

390

Calkins

NYS Thruway

390

252

253

69

16

Tinker Nature Park Trails

Location:	Calkins Road, Henrietta
Directions:	Tinker Nature Park parking area is at 1525 Calkins Road, Henrietta (between Pinnacle Road and Pittsford-Henrietta Town Line Road).
Alternate Parking:	The parking area off Pittsford-Henrietta Town Line Road
Hiking Time:	45 minutes (Perimeter Trail) 20 minutes (Nature Trail)
Length:	1.2 mile loop (Perimeter Trail) 0.5 mile loop (Nature Trail)
Difficulty:	
Surface:	Gravel path, mulched trails, and boardwalks
Trail Markings:	Some wooden signs
Uses:	
Dogs:	Pets are NOT allowed
Admission:	Free
Contact:	Tinker Nature Park 1525 Calkins Road, Pittsford, NY 14534 PO Box 999, Henrietta, NY 14467 (585) 359-7044 http://tinkernaturepark.blogspot.com/ http://hansennaturecenter.googlepages.com/
	Tinker Homestead and Farm Museum 1585 Calkins Road, Pittsford, NY 14534-2719 PO Box 999, Henrietta, NY 14467 (585) 359-7042

The land for Tinker Nature Park was donated by the Aldridge family in 1991 and made public in 1994. The well designed park has become a year-round favorite for people of all ages. It consists of woods, wetlands, ponds, and fields which together create a living museum of natural history. Within the park is the Hansen Nature Center, offering an observation beehive, nature exhibits, and classes in cross-country skiing, snowshoeing, photography, wild flowers, song birds, etc. The nature center building is open Tuesday through Saturday, 9 AM to 3:30 PM.

While there you will also want to visit the Tinker Homestead, built in 1830. This turn of the century cobblestone museum is free and open to the public, with guided tours Tuesday through Thursday and Saturdays and Sundays, noon to 4

A perfect day for a stroll at Tinker Nature Park.
Teresa Hirschman is joined by Rebecca, Ryan, and Elizabeth.

PM, other times by appointment. To explore many other unique cobblestone buildings, pick up a copy of the guidebook *Cobblestone Quest - Road Tours of New York's Historic Buildings.*

Two trails are available for hiking. Choose one or combine them for a longer hike. The Perimeter Trail has exercise stations along the way. Both trails have abundant wildlife. On a spring hike we saw nesting Canada geese, a big fat raccoon, turtles, ducks, woodpeckers, chipmunks, squirrels, and song birds too numerous to name. We listened to the music of spring peepers (a type of frog) and walked through forests carpeted with May apples.

Trail Directions — Perimeter Trail
- From the parking area follow the brick path.
- Pass the Perimeter Trail on your right. (This will be part of the return loop.)
- Pass the front of the nature center building.
- Pass the Nature Trail on the right.
- Continue on the gravel path. Pass the third trail to the right. (This also leads to the Nature Trail.) A marsh is on your left.
- At 0.2 mile, pass the Boardwalk Trail to the right. (It offers an up-close view of a pond.)
- The trail bends right and eventually heads southwest.

- Pass a trail to the left which leads to the parking area on Pittsford-Henrietta Town Line Road.
- At 0.6 mile, the Boardwalk Trail rejoins the Perimeter Trail from the right.
- A trail to the left leads to a playground area.
- Enter the woods.
- At 0.7 mile, a trail to the left leads to Pittsford-Henrietta Town Line Road. Continue straight and cross a wooden bridge.
- Wind through the woods.
- Cross bridges over a marsh area.
- Reach a junction at 1.0 mile and bear right. (Left leads to Park Acre Drive.) Cross additional bridges.
- Emerge to a grass area and a bird blind where you can observe song birds at feeders.
- Follow the split rail fence back to the nature center building.
- At the "T," turn left to return to the parking area. (Or, turn right to continue on the Nature Trail.)

Date Hiked: _____
Notes:

The boardwalk at Tinker Nature Park.

Trail Directions — Nature Trail
• From the parking area follow the brick path.
• Pass the Perimeter Trail on your right.
• Pass the front of the nature center building.
• Turn right onto the Nature Trail.
• At the "Y," bear right.
• Cross a wooden bridge.
• The trail loops left to a boardwalk over the swamp.
• At the "T," turn right.
• Meet a gravel trail and turn left.
• Pass the Nature Trail entrance on the left and the nature center building on the right.
• Bear right to return to the parking area.

Date Hiked: _____

Notes:

Genesee Valley Greenway

The Genesee Valley Greenway is an 84-mile historic and natural resource corridor which follows a transportation route that was used by the Genesee Valley Canal, from 1840 to 1878, and by the railroad, from 1880 to the mid 1960s. The former rail bed now serves as a multi-use trail open to hikers, bikers, horseback riders, cross-country skiers, and snowmobilers. The trail runs south from Rochester to the town of Cuba, with some gaps.

Two segments are described in this book. The first runs from Genesee Valley Park in Rochester to Route 383, near the airport. The second heads from Scottsville, south to Avon, or north to Route 252. Additional sections south of Avon are described in the book *Take Your Bike - Family Rides in the Finger Lakes and Genesee Valley Region.*

The Genesee Valley Greenway connects with the Rochester River Trail, the Erie Canalway Trail, the Finger Lakes Trail, as well as Rochester's Genesee Valley Park, Lehigh Valley Trail, and Letchworth State Park.

The Genesee Valley Greenway passes through wetlands, woodlands, rolling farmlands, steep gorges, historic villages, and the Genesee and Black Creek valleys. It offers something for everyone, from a short outing to a challenging long-distance trek. You can stop to explore quaint villages, visit an historic canal era inn, or inspect well-preserved stone locks and other remnants of the ingenuity and engineering that built the canal and the railroad.

This trail is a work-in-progress. Each year more mileage is opened and segments are being connected. When in doubt, follow the posted Genesee Valley Greenway signs to stay on the most recent routing of the trail.

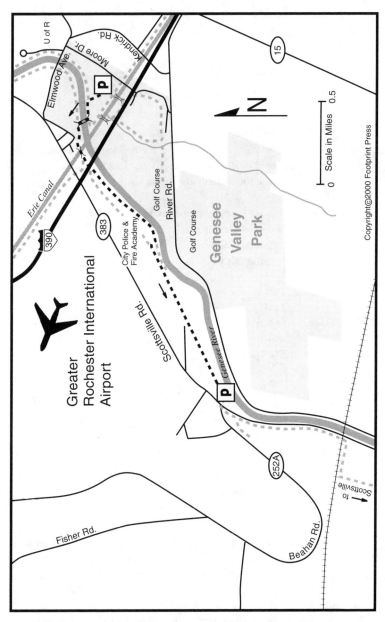

Genesee Valley Greenway - Rochester

17

Genesee Valley Greenway
- Rochester

Location:	Genesee Valley Park to Scottsville Road (Route 383)
Directions:	From Elmwood Avenue near the University of Rochester, turn southwest into Genesee Valley Park on Moore Drive. Park at the Roundhouse Pavilion parking area off Moore Drive.
Alternative Parking:	Route 383 near the intersection of Route 252A, next to Jet Diner (closed)
Hiking Time:	75 minutes one way
Length:	2.2 miles one way
Difficulty:	

Surface: Paved path

Trail Markings: Some directional signs and some "Genesee Valley Greenway" signs

Uses:

Dogs: OK on leash

Admission: Free

Contact: City of Rochester - Bureau of Parks & Recreation
400 Dewey Avenue, Rochester, NY 14613
(585) 428-6770

Friends of the Genesee Valley Greenway, Inc.
P.O. Box 42
Mount Morris, NY 14510
(585) 658-2569
www.fogvg.org

From Genesee Valley Park where the Erie Canal meets the Genesee River, follow this paved, easy-walking trail as it snakes southwest along the Genesee River heading toward Scottsville. Along the way, you'll pass the training center for Rochester police and fire units.

The trail ends at a parking area where Route 252A meets Scottsville Road (Route 383). To connect with the next segment of the Genesee Valley Greenway currently requires a short road walk south on Route 383.

Trail Directions

- From the Roundhouse parking area, head north on the paved path toward the Genesee River.
- At the "T," turn left then bear right to head uphill and cross the Waldo J. Nielson Bridge which arches over the Genesee River.
- After the bridge, turn left (NW). (To the right is the Genesee River Trail which is described in *Take Your Bike - Family Rides in the Rochester Area*.)
- At the "T," turn left to head over another bridge. This one spans the Erie Canal. (The former Pennsylvania Railroad bridge is to your right.)
- At 0.3 mile, continue straight (NW) at the next junction. (To the right is the Erie Canalway Trail to Lockport which is also described in *Take Your Bike - Family Rides in the Rochester Area*.)
- Quickly pass another trail to the right. (This is the official Genesee Valley Greenway Trail which merges shortly with the trail you're on.)
- Pass the Police & Fire Academy on your right. The Genesee River is on your left.
- At 1.0 mile, turn right just after the Academy. (Straight ahead dead-ends in 0.2 mile.)
- Pass two yellow metal gates.
- At 2.2 miles, reach the Route 383 parking area, next to the former Jet Diner. (To continue south on the Genesee Valley Greenway cross Route 383 (Scottsville Road) and turn left (W) to walk the sidewalk. Veer right onto a paved path. It will parallel the old canal bed, cross over Little Black Creek, then merge left into a parking area and canoe launch for Little Black Creek. (For this and other places to paddle, refer to *Take A Paddle - Western New York Quiet Water for Canoes & Kayaks*.) Pass through the parking area and turn right to follow the edge of Route 383 (Scottsville Road) again. Cross over the railroad tracks. Turn right (W) onto a dirt path just after the railroad tracks. Turn left onto the Genesee Valley Greenway. See the map on page 78.)

Date Hiked: _____

Notes:

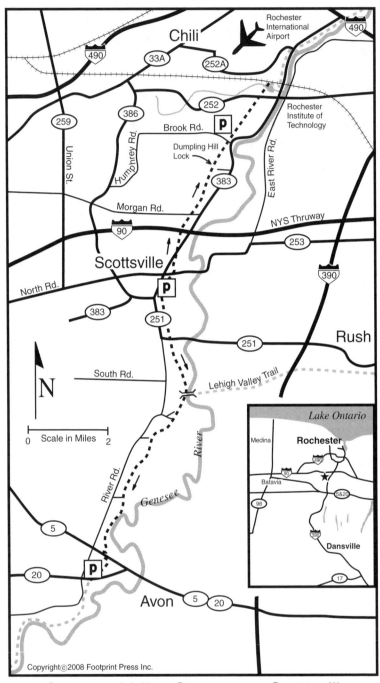

Genesee Valley Greenway - Scottsville

18

Genesee Valley Greenway
- Scottsville

Location:	Canawaugus Park, Scottsville
Directions:	From the Henrietta exit #44 on the New York State Thruway (Interstate 90), head south on Route 390. At the Route 251 exit, turn right (W) and follow Route 251 to the Canawaugus Park parking lot (on the right just before entering Scottsville and south of Oatka Creek).
Alternative Parking:	West of the trail intersection on Brook Road
Alternative Parking:	Trail intersection on Route 20
Hiking Time:	3.5 hours (north)
	4.5 hours (south)
Length:	6.6 miles one way (north)
	8.4 miles one way (south)
Difficulty:	Note: crossing Routes 5 and 383 require short inclines
Surface:	Cinder and crushed stone path
Trail Markings:	Green & white, metal "Genesee Valley Greenway" signs, small brown and yellow corridor 3 signs, and yellow metal gates at road crossings
Uses:	
Dogs:	OK on leash
Admission:	Free
Contact:	Friends of the Genesee Valley Greenway, Inc. P.O. Box 42, Mount Morris, NY 14510 (585) 658-2569 www.fogvg.org
	Regional Land Manager N.Y.S. Department of Environmental Conservation 7291 Coon Road, Bath, NY 14810 (607) 776-2165 www.dec.state.ny.us

From Canawaugus Park you can head north for 6.6 miles to the active Conrail tracks north of Route 252. This option takes you past Dumpling Hill Lock #2, one of the best-preserved locks on the Genesee Valley Canal that operated from 1840 to 1878. The canal's original 115 locks were made of either wood, a combination of

wood and stone, or all stone. Over the years, the wood rotted and most locks deteriorated or were lost altogether. But this 90-foot-long, 15-foot-wide lock is all stone and well preserved. Each lock had a lock keeper and sometimes a lock house. The Dumpling Hill Lock had a house, which was located west of the canal near Coates Road.

From the north end you can follow Route 252 east, then Route 383 north for 1.7 miles of road-walk then continue on the Genesee Valley Greenway into Genesee Valley Park. This segment is described as Trail #17 on page 75.

You can also head south from Canawaugus Park for 8.4 miles to Route 20 and beyond. This hike is more remote, passing through lush farmlands. See Trail #10 in *Take Your Bike - Family Rides in the Finger Lakes & Genesee Valley Region* for the continuation of Genesee Valley Greenway south of Route 20 for an additional 12.6 miles.

Louis D'Amanda sits atop his percheron horse, Matthew. Both enjoy an outing on a multi-use trail.

Percherons are produced by crossing Arabian horses with an old Flemish breed represented now by the Belgian.

Whichever direction you choose, the trail has an easy-hiking, hard-packed cinder or crushed stone base.

From the parking area at Canawaugus Park, look across to the north side of Oatka Creek to see an old feeder gate for the Genesee Valley Canal. A feeder gate consisted of a lock, dam, and tollhouse.

Trail Directions – North

- Follow the paved trail north and cross Oatka Creek on the plate girder (former Pennsylvania Railroad) bridge known locally as the "George Bridge." You are heading northeast on the trail. (Just north of George Bridge, a winding boardwalk to the left (called Canal Street Boardwalk) leads to the village of Scottsville.)
- Cross Route 253 and pass Rodney Farms, a thoroughbred horse farm, on the right.
- As you approach Route 383, bear right (following the Genesee Valley Greenway sign) and climb a hill.

- Cross Route 383 with care, being certain that you can see oncoming traffic far enough ahead for a safe crossing. (A short distance to the left along Route 383 is a small graveyard with the gravestone of Joseph Morgan, a Revolutionary War captain. He is credited with being the first settler in Chili in 1792.)
- Across the road, continue downhill on the trail.
- Pass under the New York State Thruway.
- Cross a gravel driveway.
- Cross Morgan Road.
- Pass under two sets of power lines.
- Cross several farm lanes.
- Reach Dumpling Hill Lock.
- Overlook horse farms as you walk high on the rail bed.
- Cross Brook Road at 4.6 miles. (The parking area is to the left down Brook Road a short distance.)
- Pass an underground gas pipeline.
- At 5.6 miles, watch for the "W" carved in a metal post on the right. It signaled the train conductor to blow the whistle as they approached a road crossing.
- Cross Ballantyne Road (Route 252). You are near the airport so don't be startled if a jet rumbles overhead.
- Pass a wetland on the right.
- You'll see Black Creek on the right as it heads toward the Genesee River. You're actually walking on a culvert where the waters of Black Creek are diverted under what used to be the Genesee Valley Canal.
- The trail ends at 6.6 miles at the active Conrail tracks. Turn around and retrace your path. (To continue north, turn right at the railroad tracks, then left along Route 383 (Scottsville Road). Cross the railroad tracks and continue north. Turn left into the Little Black Creek launch area parking lot. (For this and other places to paddle, refer to *Take A Paddle - Western New York Quiet Water for Canoes & Kayaks*.) At the far end of the parking lot, follow the dirt trail. It will become paved & loop back to Route 383. Turn left and follow Route 383 to Route 252. Cross Route 383 into the parking area for the former Jet Diner. At the back, right corner you'll find the paved trail that heads into Genesee Valley Park.)

Date Hiked: _____

Notes:

Trail Directions – South

- From the Canawaugus Park parking lot, head southwest, away from "George Bridge," on the narrow dirt double track trail.
- Cross several farm field access paths and a private driveway.
- At 1.0 mile, cross Route 251.
- Cross a bridge at 2.1 miles.
- At 2.6 miles, you'll find the intersection with the Lehigh Valley Trail where the old Lehigh Valley Railroad trestle spans the Genesee River. (Details on this trail can be found in *Take Your Bike - Family Rides in the Rochester Area*.)
- Pass an abandoned gravel pit area on the right (W).
- Cross a farm road.
- Watch carefully to see if you can find the trestle of the abandoned Peanut Branch of the New York Central Railroad. Being a small line earned it the nickname Peanut Branch.
- Pass a beaver pond.
- At 4.2 miles, cross a gated entrance to a farmer's fields labeled with a large "Warning – No Trespassing" sign.
- Cross a buried petroleum pipeline.
- Cross a road that leads to a private farm.
- Cross an underground gas pipeline and several farm lanes.
- At 7.4 miles, pass between the stone trestle of the abandoned Erie Railroad that runs east–west. (There is a path on each side.)
- Head uphill and cross Route 5.
- Across the road, head downhill.
- Pass a quarry on your right and an old segment of the Genesee River to your left. (The Genesee, like most rivers, wanders with time, leaving abandoned channels where an oxbow got cut off from the main channel.)
- Pass through yellow metal gates just before reaching Route 20 (where you can park). (The trail continues south, past Route 20.)

Date Hiked: _____

Notes:

Southeast
Section

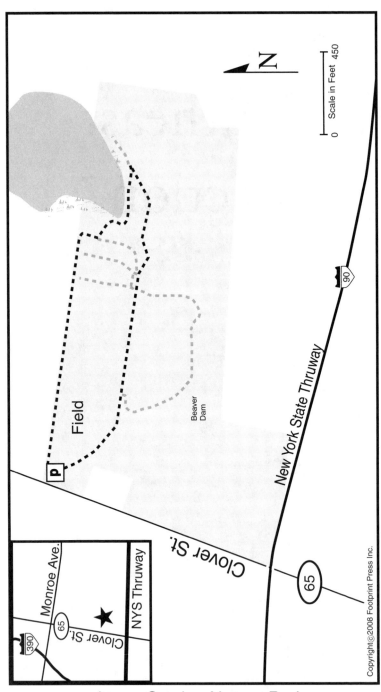

Isaac Gordon Nature Park

Field

P

Beaver
Dam

New York State Thruway

90

Clover St.

65

N

Scale in Feet

0   450

Monroe Ave.

Clover St.

65

390

NYS Thruway

19

Isaac Gordon Nature Park

Location:	Clover Street, Pittsford
Directions:	From Pittsford, head south on Route 65. The Isaac Gordon Nature Park parking area is on the east side of Clover Street (Route 65), just north of the N.Y. State Thruway.
Alternate Parking:	None
Hiking Time:	35 minutes
Length:	1.0 mile loop
Difficulty:	👢 👢 👢 👢
Surface:	Dirt and mowed-grass paths
Trail Markings:	None
Uses:	🚶 🎿
Dogs:	OK on leash
Admission:	Free
Contact:	Town of Pittsford, Parks and Recreation Department 35 Lincoln Avenue, Pittsford, NY 14534 (585) 381-8420

The Isaac Gordon Foundation and Dr. Jerome Glazer donated the land for this delightful park to the town of Pittsford. The western section is a farm field that the trail circumnavigates. The eastern section is a pond and wetland in a hilly forest. In May the forest floor is dotted with groves of trillium. Making a series of loops around the various intersecting paths can extend your enjoyment of this park. This is a great bird watching park.

Trail Directions

• From the parking area walk south on the mulched trail. It will take you to a treed tunnel with a canopy of leaves overhead.
• Continue straight, past a trail to the right. (The 0.3-mile path to the right meanders through a mowed field and circles back to meet the treed tunnel. You can extend your hike another 5 minutes by turning right but the field is uneven, difficult to walk, and can be wet.)
• Continue straight through the next intersection.
• Continue straight, past a grassy trail to the left.
• The trail will head uphill and bend left several times, then heads downhill.

- At 0.5 mile, turn left and head downhill. (The path straight ahead dead-ends shortly. It is however, a nice walk through woods on a narrow path along the wetland.)
- Wind through the woods with the wetlands to your right.
- Continue uphill. Turn right (N) when the path comes to a "T."
- Pass two trails off to the left (or loop back to extend your walk) and continue straight to return to the parking area.

Date Hiked: _____

Notes:

Mendon Ponds Park

This is a jewel in the county's park system, filled with lakes, woods, and rolling hills. Mendon Ponds Park is the largest park in Monroe County and was designated a National Natural Landmark because of its unique glacial land forms.

The park's geologic features were formed by the last of four major glaciers that covered the area 12,000 to 14,000 years ago. The glacier reached to the Pennsylvania border and was 5,000 to 10,000 feet thick. As the ice melted, large amounts of sand, rock, and gravel were deposited. Three main geologic features visible in the park today are: kames, eskers, and kettles.

Kames — formed by rivers that flowed on top of the glacier and spilled over the edge depositing soil into huge piles.

KAME

Eskers — formed when rivers flowed under the glacier in an ice tunnel. Rocky material accumulated on the tunnel beds, and when the glacier melted, a ridge of rubble remained.

ESKER

Kettles — created when a large block of ice separated from the glacier. Water running off of the glacier deposited gravel and debris all around the ice block. The block melted, leaving behind a rough circular depression.

KETTLE

People from all over the country come to study "Devil's Bathtub." This kettle is a rare meromictic lake, of which there are only a few in the world. A meromictic lake is a very deep body of water surrounded by high ridges. Because the high ridges prevent the wind from blowing on the water, the lake's water levels never turn over and the motionless surface gives the lake a mirrored effect.

The first inhabitants of this area were the Algonquin, Iroquois, and Seneca Indians who left behind many Indian trails. On July 23, 1687, the Marquis de Denonville's army used the trails to attack the Indians in the region. In his memoirs, Denonville recalls looking down from the top of one of the ridges at "three pretty little lakes." The first reference to Mendon Ponds in our recorded history.

The first white settler in the Mendon Ponds area was Joshua Lillie, who is buried on a small plot on Wilmarth Road. The park was dedicated in 1928 and now has 25 to 30 miles of winding trails.

Wild Wings runs a raptor rehabilitation center near the Nature Center on Pond Road in Mendon Ponds Park. They are open to the public every day from 10:00 AM until 2:00 PM except Wednesdays, Thursdays and holidays.

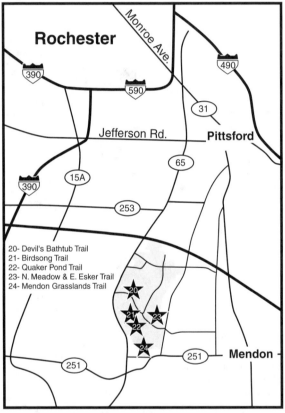

20- Devil's Bathtub Trail
21- Birdsong Trail
22- Quaker Pond Trail
23- N. Meadow & E. Esker Trail
24- Mendon Grasslands Trail

Trails in Mendon Ponds Park

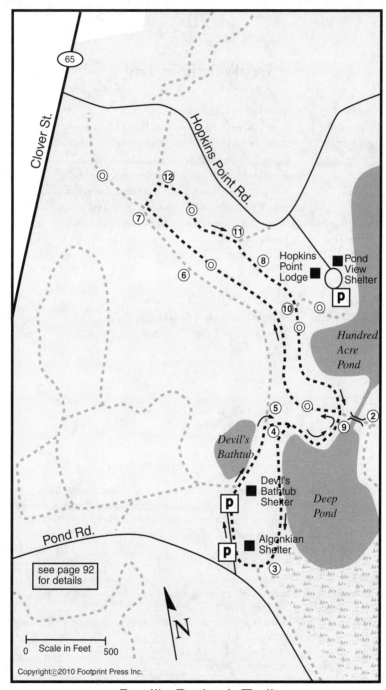

Devil's Bathtub Trail

20

Devil's Bathtub Trail

Location:	Mendon Ponds Park, Mendon
Directions:	From Rochester head south on Route 65 (Clover Street). Turn left (E) at the third entrance to Mendon Ponds Park on Pond Road. Turn left just before Algonkian Shelter and park in the Devil's Bathtub Shelter parking area. (When this access road is closed in winter, park at the Algonkian Shelter parking area.)
Alternative Parking:	Algonkian Shelter parking area along Pond Road
Hiking Time:	1 hour and 15 minutes
Length:	2.3 mile loop
Difficulty:	🦶 🦶 🦶 🦶
Surface:	Dirt and mulched path
Trail Markings:	Some blue numbered signs on posts
	Most of the trail is orange blazed
Uses:	🚶
Dogs:	OK on leash
Admission:	Free
Contact:	Monroe County Parks Department
	171 Reservoir Avenue
	Rochester, NY 14620
	(585) 256-4950
	www.monroecounty.gov/parks-index.php

The route described will introduce you to the variety of Mendon Ponds Park. It begins with a descent to Devil's Bathtub kettle pond, nestled in a deep valley. Then you'll climb steeply to the ridge of an esker. Descend off the esker to walk through a wooded forest valley then wander a flat trail along the edge of Hundred Acre Pond and Deep Pond.

Trail Directions

- From the Devil's Bathtub Shelter parking area, walk under the wooden "Mendon NYS-YCC-1989 Devil's Bathtub Trail" sign.
- Descend the wooden stairs and continue straight on the boardwalk with Devil's Bathtub kettle pond to your left.
- Bear right (E) when the trail "Y's" and head uphill.
- Quickly, bear right again and continue uphill.

- Continue straight (SE) through an intersection and head downhill to Deep Pond. (Pass additional small trails along the way.)
- At 0.2 mile, reach a "T" and turn left. Deep Pond is now on your right.
- Pass an opening to Deep Pond on the right.
- At the next trail junction, turn left and head uphill. This is a long climb to the ridge of the esker.
- Reach the top of the esker and continue straight on the wide trail.
- Continue straight (N) passing several small trails on both sides.
- At 0.7 mile you'll see junction marker #10 where the trail "Y's." Bear left to continue on the esker ridge.
- Reach a trail intersection at 1.0 mile (marker #7) and turn right (E) to descend off the esker.
- At 1.1 miles, reach junction marker #12 and turn right (SE) to continue downhill.
- Continue straight (S) passing a trail to the left. Junction marker #11 is buried in the bushes at this junction.
- At 1.4 miles continue straight through the intersection marked with junction marker #8.
- Quickly pass another trail to the right. Stay on the main trail and head downhill to pond level.
- At the "T," turn right (SW). Hundred Acre Pond is now on your left.
- Pass a small trail to the right.
- At 1.7 miles, continue straight (SW) past a trail to the left that leads between the ponds.
- Pass junction marker #9 and a trail to the right. Continue straight (SW) following orange blazes.
- Pass an opening to Deep Pond on the left.
- Pass two trails on the right.
- At 2.1 miles, reach Algonkian Shelter. Turn right and pass the shelter.
- Turn right at the access road, passing a metal yellow gate. Head uphill to the Devil's Bathtub Shelter parking area.

Date Hiked: _____

Notes:

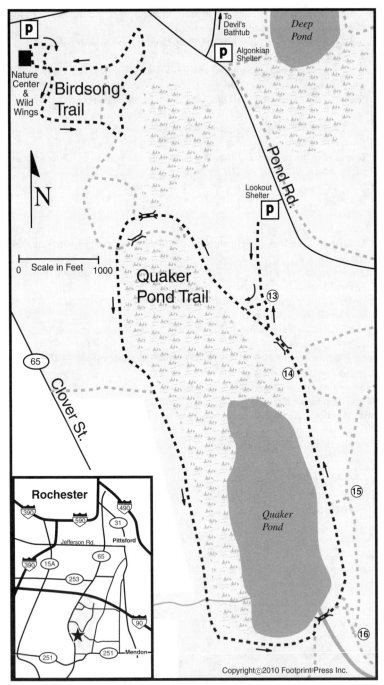

Birdsong Trail & Quaker Pond Trail

21

Birdsong Trail

Location:	Mendon Ponds Park, Mendon
Directions:	From Rochester, head south on Route 65 (Clover Street). At the third park entrance, turn left into Mendon Ponds Park on Pond Road. The nature center parking area will be on the right.
Alternative Parking:	None
Hiking Time:	35 minutes
Length:	1.1 mile loop
Difficulty:	🥾 🥾 🥾
Surface:	Dirt path
Trail Markings:	Signs at intersections
Uses:	🚶
Dogs:	Pets are NOT allowed
Admission:	Free
Contact:	Monroe County Parks Department 171 Reservoir Avenue Rochester, NY 14620 (585) 256-4950 www.monroecounty.gov/parks-index.php

As the name indicates, many birds populate this area especially black-capped chickadees. These friendly, curious creatures will fly right up to you, and if you have sunflower seeds, they will eat out of your hand. For part of the journey, you'll walk an old farm lane as evidenced by the large trees that line the trail. Some of them are labeled, making this walk an arbor study.

Black-capped chickadees
eat from your hand.

Near the parking lot, be sure to visit Wild Wings. It is a not-for-profit educational organization that houses and cares for permanently injured birds of prey (raptors), which are unable to survive on their own in the wild any more. The exhibits are open to the public every day from 10:00 AM to 2:00 PM except Wednesdays, Thursdays and holidays.

Trail Directions

- From the trellis walkway, turn left on Old Orchard Trail.
- The trail will bend right.
- At the "T," turn left onto an old farm lane.
- Quickly turn right onto Birdsong Trail. (Notice the stone walls that line both sides of the trail. Imagine the farmer who had to clear these from his fields.)
- At 0.2 mile the trail bends left at a sign about animal tracks.
- Turn right at the "T."
- Reach a "Y" at 0.4 mile and bear left on Birdsong Trail.
- Pass two small trails to the right. (They lead to a small swamp with an observation deck and benches.)
- Pass an observation deck at 0.5 mile.
- Pass a bench and head downhill beside a wooden railing. There's a second bench at the bottom of the hill.
- Reach a "T" at 0.9 mile and turn right (NW).
- Continue straight, passing a trail to the left then another to the right.
- Pass an observation platform on the left and bear right on a paved path toward the nature center building.
- Pass a hummingbird garden, a butterfly garden, and an herb garden.
- Turn right to head under the trellis and return to the parking area.

Dorothy Murphy and
Joyce Connor stroll
along Birdsong Trail.

Date Hiked: _____

Notes:

94

22

Quaker Pond Trail

Location:	Mendon Ponds Park, Mendon
Directions:	Take Clover Street (Route 65) south to Mendon Ponds Park. Turn left (E) at the third entrance to the park on Pond Road. Pass the nature center and Algonkian Shelter. Park at the Lookout Shelter parking area.
Alternative Parking:	The nature center parking area
Hiking Time:	1.3 hours
Length:	2.5 mile loop
Difficulty:	👣 👣 👣 👣
Surface:	Mowed-grass and dirt path
Trail Markings:	Some signs and numbered posts at intersections
Uses:	🚶 ⛷
Dogs:	Pets are NOT allowed
Admission:	Free
Contact:	Monroe County Parks Department
	171 Reservoir Avenue
	Rochester, NY 14620
	(585) 256-4950
	www.monroecounty.gov/parks-index.php

This trail offers an easy stroll on a wide path. Cattails and bushes are encroaching on the pond, but water is still visible at the southern end. Waterfowl and lily pads are plentiful in the remaining pond. In spring and winter it's a fun place to identify animal tracks (deer, raccoon, beaver, etc.) in the mud. On a winter walk we watched a mink scurry across the ice. In July we've enjoyed grazing on the raspberries and blackberries that line the trail.

You can make the hike longer by combining this walk with Birdsong Trail (#21) or Mendon Grasslands Trail (#24).

Trail Directions

- From Lookout Shelter parking area, head west on the gravel trail. Immediately turn left (S).
- At the "Y," (junction marker #13) bear right (W).
- At 0.2 mile, reach a "T." Turn right (W).
- At 0.4 mile, pass a trail to the left. (It's a boardwalk through the swamp and can be taken as a shortcut.)
- Bear left as you pass a trail to the right.

- Pass a bench and cross a small wooden bridge over the swamp outlet.
- At 0.5 mile, a trail to the right leads to the nature center. Continue straight (W).
- Continue straight through a trail intersection.
- At 0.8 mile, pass a trail to the right. (It leads to Clover Street.)
- Cross a culvert at 1.4 miles.
- At 1.5 miles the trail bends left (SE).
- Pass a trail to the right.
- At the "T," turn left (E). Finally you'll see water.
- Cross a wooden bridge over the pond outlet at 1.7 miles.

Sunset over Quaker Pond.

(Notice that beavers had once dammed this waterway.)
- At the "Y," bear left (NE).
- Pass a trail to the right at 1.8 miles.
- At 2.0 miles pass a trail to the left then quickly pass a trail to the right.
- At 2.3 miles reach trail junction #14. Continue straight.
- Cross a small wooden bridge.
- At 2.3 miles, bear right (N) at the "Y" to head back to Lookout Hill and Pond Road.
- Reach a "T" at junction marker #13 at 2.4 miles and turn right (NE).
- At the last "T" turn right to return to the parking area.

Date Hiked: _____

Notes:

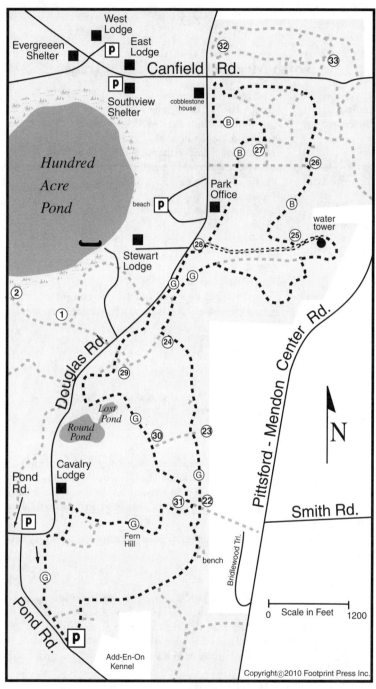

West
Lodge
Evergreeen
Shelter
East
Lodge
P
Canfield Rd.
32
33
P
Southview
Shelter
cobblestone
house
Hundred
Acre
Pond
B
beach P
Park
Office
B
27
26
B
water
tower
25
28
Stewart
Lodge
2
G
G
1
24
Douglas Rd.
29
Lost
Pond
G
Round
Pond
30
23
Cavalry
Lodge
G
Pond
Rd.
31
22
P
G
Fern
Hill
bench
Bridlewood Trl.
G
Smith Rd.
Pittsford - Mendon Center Rd.
N
Pond Rd.
P
0   Scale in Feet   1200
Add-En-On
Kennel
Copyright©2010 Footprint Press Inc.

North Meadow & East Esker Trails

23

North Meadow & East Esker Trails

Location:	Mendon Ponds Park, Mendon
Directions:	From Route 65, turn east into Mendon Ponds Park on Pond Road. Pass Douglas Road and park in the "Horse Trailer Parking" area on the north side of Pond Road, just before Add-En-On Kennel.
Alternative Parking:	The parking area at the corner of Pond Road and Douglas Road
	Along Canfield Road, east of Douglas Road
Hiking Time:	3 hours
Length:	5.7 mile loop
Difficulty:	🥾 🥾 🥾 🥾
Surface:	Dirt and mulched path
Trail Markings:	Not well marked, some blue and white metal signs on wooden posts at trail junctions, as well as some green and blue blazes
Uses:	🚶 🐎 🎿
Dogs:	OK on leash
Admission:	Free
Contact:	Monroe County Parks Department
	171 Reservoir Avenue, Rochester, NY 14620
	(585) 256-4950
	www.monroecounty.gov/parks-index.php

This wide, distinctively hilly path is used for cross-country skiing in the winter and hiking and horseback riding the rest of the year. The trail is well maintained with mulch in heavy wear areas making it an easy-to-hike horse trail. You're likely to encounter horses on a nice weekend day and need to be alert for fresh horse droppings year-round.

There are many opportunities to shorten the loop hike, if you wish. Simply refer to the map.

Trail Directions
- From the Pond Road parking area with the brown "Horse Trailer Parking" sign, head north on the farm lane. (A trail to the right goes to Add-En-On Kennel.)
- Continue uphill on the main path avoiding the cut-off on the left. Go up and over the crest of the hill and cross through a valley.
- At the top of the next hill is a tiny loop with a view and bench. Continue north along the top of the esker.
- Continue straight past a trail to the left.

- Reach a "T" and turn right. Notice the sign "Duck Hill" on the tree to your right.
- At the 5-way junction continue straight, following the wide green-blazed trail. (Note: a horse trail parallels and crosses the hiking trail a few times.)
- At the top of the next hill signed "Hawk Hill," pass junction marker #23 and continue straight following the green blazes.
- At the "T," find marker #24. Bear right and ascend and then descend an esker.
- Continue straight, downhill at the junction marked with a 14E orienteering stake.

The deer of Mendon Ponds Park.

- Pass a trail on the left. Continue straight (SE) through a small trail intersection from the right, then one from the left.
- Stay right on the wide, mulched path as it climbs a steep hill and leads to the water tower at 2.2 miles. (Note: both trails lead to the water tower.)
- The path continues on the opposite side of the tower using a gravel road for a short distance.
- At junction marker #25, turn right (N) on a blue-blazed trail.
- Pass a park bench on the left.
- Reach junction #26 and bear right.
- Pass a side trail on the right.
- At the top of the hill continue straight past a trail to the right.
- For the next several junctions always bear left to stay on the dirt trail, paralleling Canfield Road, and follow the trail to Douglas Rd.
- Turn left (S) at Douglas Road and walk the mowed grass area passing a cobblestone house. To learn more about cobblestone houses, read *Cobblestone Quest - Road Tours of New York's Historic Buildings.*
- Turn left (E) and pass an "Authorized Vehicles Only" sign.
- A trail enters from the left, continue straight.
- At the next junction turn right at the orienteering marker 9M, following blue blazes.
- Pass trees planted in rows.
- Go straight when a trail crosses, (marked by "Tree Walk #6").
- Emerge from the woods behind the park office and then reenter, continuing on the blue-blazed path.
- Bear right at the "Y," and turn right onto the gravel road (which leads left to the water tower.) Turn left at the gated fence, near marker #28.
- After several hills, enter a grass area following the edge of the woods and reenter the woods, now on the green-blazed trail.
- Cross another grass area.
- Bear right toward Douglas Road. A grass trail heads off to the left.
- Continue following the defined trail around the swamp on the left.

Mendon Pond Park's East Esker Trail.

- A short-cut trail merges from the right.
- Climb the hill up to 3 posts. Bear right.
- The short-cut trail from the right merges.
- The trail bends left as you approach Douglas Road.
- At the grassy opening, bear left between posts around Lost Pond, returning into the woods.
- Reach junction marker #30 and continue straight. (The path is leaf covered and the terrain is gentle through this area.)
- Pass a small trail junction.
- At junction marker #31, turn right and head uphill (W). The terrain becomes hilly again.
- At the next junction, go straight, downhill.
- A small trail comes in straight ahead. Bear right and head uphill following green blazes.
- Pass the "Fern Hill" sign.
- Pass two trails to the left. Bear right, following green blazes.
- The green trail turns left just before Calvary Lodge.
- Pass a gravel and sand hillside.
- At the "T," turn right (W).
- The trail bears left at Douglas Road and reenters the woods, heading uphill.
- Continue straight past a trail to the left, and return to the parking lot.

Date Hiked: _____
Notes:

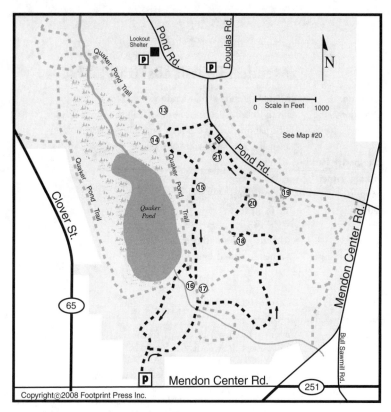

Mendon Grasslands Trail

24

Mendon Grasslands Trail

Location:	Mendon Ponds Park, Mendon
Directions:	From Route 65 turn east onto Mendon Center Road. The parking area is 0.3 mile from the corner. Look for a small brown and white horse sign.
Alternative Parking:	Along Pond Road
Hiking Time:	1.25 hours
Length:	3.4 mile loop
Difficulty:	🥾 🥾 🥾
Surface:	Mowed-grass and dirt trails
Trail Markings:	Some numbered sign posts
Uses:	
Dogs:	Pets are NOT allowed
Admission:	Free
Contact:	Monroe County Parks Department 171 Reservoir Avenue, Rochester, NY 14620 (585) 256-4950 www.monroecounty.gov/parks-index.php

Enter Mendon Ponds Park through its back door into a secluded area of rolling hills, young forests, scrub brush, and large grass fields. Horses are allowed on most of this route, but the trails are in good shape for hiking and are wide enough to avoid the horse trough where it does exist.

You'll walk through fields of tall grasses and along Quaker Pond to the serenade of Canada geese, and evidence of beaver activity. We walked this trail in early spring when ice still covered portions of the pond and were treated to mink playing on the ice and a blue heron patiently waiting to catch his dinner. Be sure to bring some sunflower seeds. The Chickadees lay in wait along this trail, expecting a hand-out. They're bold enough to land on your hand to get the seeds.

Trail Directions
- From the parking area on Mendon Center Road, head north on an eight-foot-wide mowed path.
- Enter the woods and bear right at the "Y" on the horse trail.
- Leave the woods and bear left, passing a trail to the right. Stay on the wide trail.
- Pass another small trail to the right.
- At 0.4 mile, cross Quaker Pond outlet.
- At junction marker #17 take a sharp right, heading east.

- At 0.7 mile, pass the entrance to a small, high-water loop trail on the left. (If the trail has been muddy, take this high-water route to the left.)
- Pass the return of the high-water loop.
- At 1.0 mile reach a "T" and turn right (E).
- Turn right (N) at junction marker #18.
- Continue straight (N) through junction marker #20.
- At the next intersection (shortly before the road), turn left (NW) and head uphill. Notice the remains of an old brick outhouse at the top of the hill in a grove of trees.
- Pass a trail to a parking area on the right then quickly bear right past two trails to the left. You're now heading north.
- Walk along the edge of Pond Road for about 50 feet then turn left (SW) into a gully.
- Pass a small pond on the right.
- Take the first left (SE) before the "No Horses" sign on junction marker #14 and head uphill. This is a good place to stop and feed Chickadees from your hand.
- At 2.3 miles, reach a "T" and turn right (SW).
- At the next junction, bear left and pass junction marker #15 hidden in brush to the left.
- At the next junction, turn right (W). (If you go to far you'll reach junction marker #16. Just turn right and backtrack.)
- Quickly pass through an intersection and continue straight (W) toward Quaker Pond.
- At the "T," turn left (W) along the edge of Quaker Pond. Notice all the trees cut by beavers as you approach the outlet bridge.
- Cross the wooden outlet bridge. You've come 2.8 miles.
- Continue straight (S), past a trail to the right.
- Pass a barricade and continue straight to return to the parking area.

Date Hiked: _____

Notes:

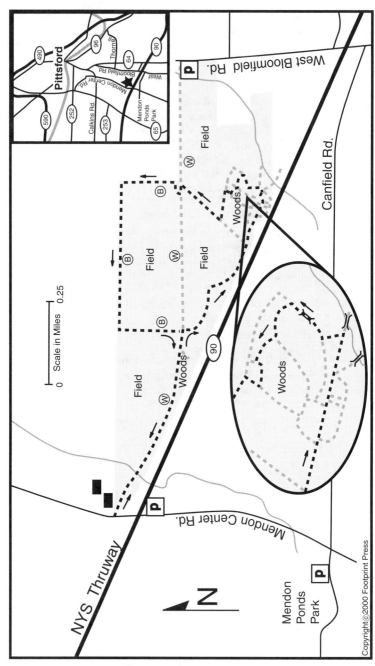

Royal Coach Trail

25

Royal Coach Trail

Location:	Mendon Center Road, Pittsford
Directions:	From Pittsford, head south on Route 64. Bear right onto Mendon Center Road. Parking is not allowed at the trailhead. Park along Mendon Center Road just south of the NYS Thruway overpass.
Alternative Parking:	Along Canfield Road in Mendon Ponds Park
	A gravel pull-off area along West Bloomfield Road
Hiking Time:	75 minutes
Length:	2.2 mile loop
Difficulty:	👣 👣 👣
Surface:	Mowed-grass and dirt trails
Trail Markings:	White and blue blazes
Uses:	🚶 🎿 🐎
Dogs:	OK on leash
Admission:	Free
Contact:	Pittsford Parks & Recreation
	35 Lincoln Avenue, Pittsford, NY 14534
	(585) 248-6280

Royal Coach gets its name from Walnut Hill Farms which abuts the property on the eastern edge. Each August, Walnut Hill is the meeting place for elaborate horse drawn coaches and carts. They host a competition of driving skill and give awards for costuming and restoration of the old carriages. Watching the competition is a fun way to spend a summer weekend day. The horses and carts use the trails through the woods at the eastern end of this property for their time trials.

On a fall day, while walking on Royal Coach Trail, we were treated to a rare sight. A young gray fox pranced in front of us and pounced several times as he hunted for mice in the fields. We were down wind so it was only when we crept forward to get a better look that he took note of us and bounded away.

The trail begins with a climb past farm fields. Once at the top of the hill you enter a maze of trails in a deep woods. This is where the driving competition takes place. Sometimes there are wooden sculptures or trees with eyes and mustaches on them in the woods. The return winds downhill around fields.

The drone of Thruway noise is never out of earshot, but the splendor of hilltop vistas makes it bearable. In fall, the reds, bronzes, yellows, and greens of the trees contrast sharply with the beige carpet of dying cornstalks. This is indeed a pretty place to go for a stroll.

Trail Directions
- Follow Mendon Center Road north, passing under the NYS Thruway bridge.
- Less than 0.1 mile from the Thruway bridge, turn right (E) at the green "Town of Pittsford Parkland Restrictions" sign.
- Walk east on a farm lane. It parallels the Thruway and heads uphill.
- Pass another green sign at 0.3 mile as a woods begins to your right.
- A small path to the right leads into woods. Continue straight until a gap in the woods on your right.

Boulder leads Dave Wright, Dave Coleman, and Rich Freeman on a fall hike on Royal Coach Trail.

- Turn right and follow the mowed-grass trail around the edge of a field toward the Thruway. (You're on an unmarked trail.)
- Parallel the thruway then proceed straight (E).
- Pass a grassy trail to the left and continue straight (E) entering the woods at 0.7 mile. (The woods are full of many intersecting trails.)
- Continue straight on the wide path. (You'll pass a trail to the left, then a trail to the right.)
- Keep going straight. (You'll pass a trail on the left then 3 trails to the right. The third right leads over a small bridge.)
- At 0.8 mile turn left (N) and head uphill. (If you miss this turn you'll cross a bridge over a small creek. This is private property so turn around.)
- Reach a "T" and turn right (NE).
- Cross a wooden bridge then bear left to stay in the woods. (Straight leads to a field.)
- At 0.9 mile, reach a "Y." Bear right (N).
- Reach a "T." Turn left and follow the trail as it winds through the woods. (Right leads to a field.)
- Reach another "T." This time turn right (N) to leave the woods. (Left passes the pine tree carving.)
- At the field, turn left and follow the edge of the field (NW).
- At 1.1 miles, reach a wide "T" and turn right (NE) on a wide grass strip between fields.
- Reach a "T" and gas line post #85. Turn left (NW). (Right leads to West Bloomfield Road.)
- Quickly turn right (N) on the blue-blazed trail. (The trail winds through wooded hedge rows.)
- Bear left twice, following the blue blazes, then head downhill.

- At 1.6 miles, bear left again then head uphill.
- Reach a wide mowed "T" at 1.7 miles and turn right (NW) between the woods and a field.
- Follow the farm road back down to Mendon Center Road.
- Turn left to return to your car.

Date Hiked: _____

Notes:

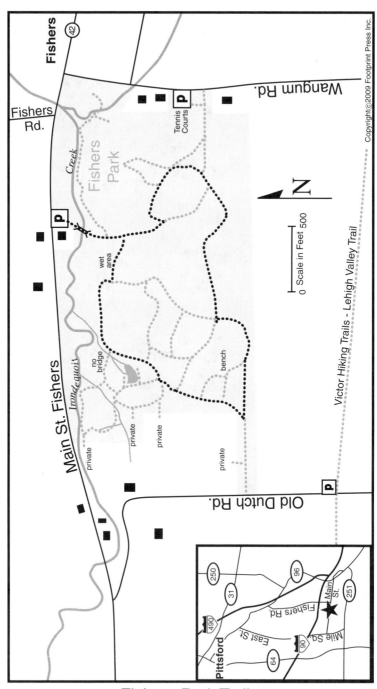

Fishers Park Trail

26

Fishers Park Trail

Location:	Fishers Park, Main Street, Fishers
Directions:	From Route 96, head west on Main Street, Fishers, just south of the Thruway. The Fishers Park parking area will be on the left, past Wangum Road.
	N43o 0.564 - W77o 28.417
Alternate Parking:	At the tennis courts on Wangum Road
	N43o 0.410 - W77o 28.226
Hiking Time:	1 hour loop
Length:	1.6-mile loop (darkened trail)
	3.2 miles total trails
Difficulty:	👣 👣 👣
Surface:	Dirt and mowed-grass paths
Trail Markings:	None
Uses:	🚶 🎿
Dogs:	OK on leash
Contact:	Town of Victor
	85 East Main Street, Victor, NY 14564
	(585) 924-7141
	Victor Hiking Trails
	85 East Main Street, Victor, NY 14564-1397
	(585) 234-8226
	www.victorhikingtrails.org

Fishers Park was part of the original Fisher homestead where pioneer Charles Fisher prospered by clearing the forest, sawing the lumber in his mills and selling the cleared land to farmers. The next generation of Fishers, brothers William and Henry Pardee Fisher, operated a nursery here, specializing in newly developed varieties of apples and pears, per William's grandson, J. Sheldon Fisher at a park dedication ceremony in 2001. The western part of the park, which is rolling grasslands today, was pasture land for cattle and sheep and still contains several fast-flowing springs.

In 1927, J. Sheldon Fisher used white-washed stones to spell out "Fishers," 110-feet-long and 10-feet-high on the hilltop to help early

Historical photo of painted stones helping early pilots find
their way to Rochester. (Photo courtesy of Larry Fisher.)

bi-plane pilots find their way to Rochester. Some white stones can still be
found on the hill above the present day tennis courts.

The dedication ceremony, where J. Sheldon Fisher spoke, commemo-
rated the expansion of Fishers Park. In 2001 Chauncy Young (a founding
and active member of Victor Hiking Trails) sold 54 acres of land to the
Town of Victor at far below market price to preserve his cherished land for-
ever and make it available to the public. A 37.5-acre park became a 59-acre
park.

Within this park, picnic tables and charcoal grills can be found at the
Main Street entrance, a baseball field at the corner, and tennis courts off
Wangum Road. Fisherman frequent the banks of Irondequoit Creek which
flows through the park.

The trail described will take you across the Irondequoit Creek valley and
up the facing hillside, deep within a peaceful woods. Then you'll swing
west to enjoy the beautiful rolling grassland hills at the western end of the
park. Sit for awhile and absorb the beauty of nature at the bench com-
memorating Melissa Young, Chauncy Young's daughter.

Trail Directions
- From the Fishers Park parking area, head toward the "Trail head" sign
  and cross Irondequoit Creek on a bridge.
- Head uphill through the woods, and pass a trail to the left.
- Turn left onto the second left side trail.
- Take one of the trails to the right, then turn right when it ends.
- Turn left at the next junction.
- Emerge from the woods and turn left on the grassland trails.
- Take the second right on the mowed-grass trails.

- Take the forth right.
- Then take the second left onto a narrow trail through a low, wet area in the woods.
- When it meets the main trail, turn left to return to the parking area.

Date Hiked: _____

Notes:

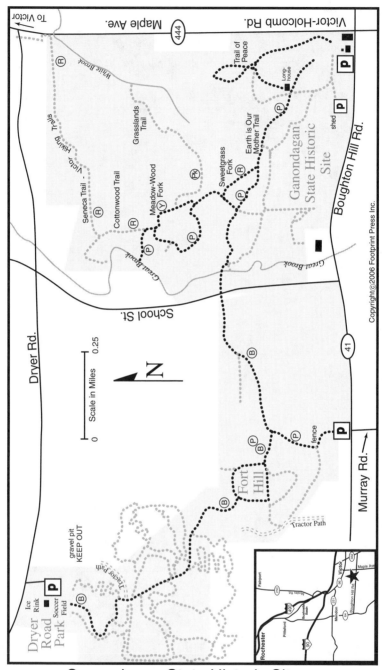

Ganondagan State Historic Site
& Dryer Road Park

27

Ganondagan State Historic Site / Dryer Road Park

Location: Ganondagan State Historic Site, Boughton Hill Road,
               Victor, Ontario County
Directions: From Route 96 in Victor, turn south on Maple Avenue
               (State Route 444) then west on Boughton Hill Road
               (County Road 41), Ganondagan parking lot is on
               Boughton Hill Road near the corner of Victor-
               Holcomb Road. N42º 57.685 - W77º 24.788
Alternative Parking: A parking area near the shed off Boughton Hill
               Road. N42º 57.6800 - W77º 24.8447
Alternative Parking: The Fort Hill parking area on Boughton Hill Road.
               N42º 57.670 - W77º 25.924
Uses:

Dogs: OK on leash
Contact: Ganondagan State Historic Site
               P.O. Box 239, 1488 Victor-Holcomb Road
               Victor, NY 14564-0239
               (585) 924-5848
               www.ganondagan.org

Once a major seventeenth-century Seneca town and its palisaded gra-
nary, Ganondagan is the only historic site, under the auspices of New York
State Office of Parks, Recreation and Historic Preservation, that is dedicated to Native Americans. The town and its associated burial grounds on
Boughton Hill were designated a National Historic Landmark in 1964.
Fort Hill, the site of the town's granary, was placed on the National
Register of Historic Places in 1966 because it was part of the French campaign of destruction in 1687. The Marquis de Denonville, Governor
General of New France, led an army of 3,000 men from Canada against
the Seneca in July, 1687, in an effort to annihilate the Seneca and eliminate
them as competitors in the international fur trade.

The Seneca recall a much earlier time period, when a man referred to as
the Peacemaker journeyed to their territory and met a woman known as
Mother of Nations or Peace Mother. The Seneca know Ganondagan as the
"Town of Peace," and revere and protect the burial site of the Mother of
Nations near here.

The Seneca Indian longhouse at Ganondagan.

Interpretive signs on the three main trails within Ganondagan teach the significance of plant life for the Seneca, Seneca customs and beliefs, features of the 30 acre granary at Fort Hill, and the events that took place at the granary. On July 14, 1987, Ganondagan was dedicated — 300 years to the day after Denonville destroyed life at Ganondagan.

In 1997 and 1998 a full-scale bark longhouse was constructed at Ganondagan based on extensive research of oral, archaeological, and historical records. The 65-foot long, 20-foot wide structure is stocked with artifacts and displays, showing not only how the Seneca lived, but their governmental and spiritual philosophies as well. When the peaceful Seneca inhabited Ganondagan, up to 20 families could have lived in each longhouse. Ganondagan was the largest Seneca town known to have existed. In the 17th century it had over 150 longhouses and approximately 4,500 residents. Hours that the longhouse is open for viewing vary throughout the year. Call (585) 924-5848 for the current schedule.

The visitor center at Ganondagan features an exhibit describing the Seneca clan system, a display of works by Seneca artists, and a twenty-seven minute video about the history of Ganondagan. The visitor center and gift shop are open May 1 through September 30, Tuesday through Sunday, 9 AM to 5 PM and during October, Tuesday through Saturday, 9 AM to 5 PM. Admission to the visitor center and longhouse costs $3/adult and $2/child. Self-guided walks on the trails are free.

There are many options for walks at Ganondagan State Historic Site. Four options are described starting on the following page:

Trail of Peace

Hiking Time:	15 minute loop
Length:	0.4-mile loop
Difficulty:	👟
Surface:	Mowed-grass path
Trail Markings:	None

Stay on top of the hill and walk the undulating mowed-grass paths of the Trail of Peace through open fields for an easy 0.4-mile loop, and visit the replica longhouse.

Trail Directions
- From the parking area head north through the opening in the split-rail fence to cross a mowed-grass area toward a sign "Trail of Peace."
- Visit the longhouse, then continue north on the mowed-grass loop trails, passing interpretive signs.

Date Hiked: _____

Notes:

Earth Is Our Mother Trail

Hiking Time:	1.0 hour loop
Length:	1.9-mile loop
Difficulty:	👟 👟 👟
Surface:	Dirt path with boardwalks
Trail Markings:	Colored metal markers

Head into the woods for the more challenging Earth is Our Mother Trail.

Trail Directions
- From the parking area head north through the opening in the split-rail fence to cross a mowed-grass area toward a sign "Trail of Peace."
- Pass the longhouse. Head into the woods behind it, passing the silver and black "Ethnobotanical Trail" sign.

115

•Follow the purple marked trail outbound to Great Brook and take the yellow (Meadow-Wood Fork) and red (Sweetgrass Fork) marked segments on the return.

Date Hiked: _____

Notes:

Looking south from atop Fort Hill.

Fort Hill Trail

Directions:	The grass parking area for Fort Hill will be on the north side of Boughton Hill Road near the corner of Murray Road. N42º 57.670 - W77º 25.924
Hiking Time:	30 minutes to hike (1 hour to hike & read the signs)
Length:	1-mile loop
Difficulty:	👣 👣 👣
Surface:	Dirt and mowed-grass paths
Trail Markings:	Parts of the trail are marked purple & blue

The Fort Hill Trail takes you to the top of a plateau with sweeping views of valleys and hillsides across Victor. This was once the site of the picketed granary for Ganondagan where the winter supply of corn was stored. Forty interpretive signs give first-hand accounts of the mass destruction of the granary by the French campaign of 1687.

Trail Directions

• From the parking area head uphill (N) on the mowed path.
• Turn right and enter the woods through wooden fence posts.
• At 0.2 mile, cross a boardwalk. (To your left note the marsh area, once a spring used by the Seneca.)
• Turn left at the blue trail junction.
• At the top of the plateau, head either direction to walk the perimeter of the clearing. Read the interpretive signs along the way, and sit and enjoy the views of farmland in the valley below.
• Return to the parking area, downhill, via the same trail.

Date Hiked: _____

Notes:

Traverse to Dryer Road Park

Location:	Ganondagan State Historic Site on Boughton Hill Road to Dryer Road Park on Dryer Road, Victor, Ontario County
Directions:	From Route 96 in Victor, turn south on Maple Avenue (State Route 444), then west on Boughton Hill Road (County Road 41). Ganondagan parking lot is on Boughton Hill Road near the corner of Victor-Holcomb Road. N42º 57.685 - W77º 24.788
Alternative Parking:	Dryer Road Park on the south side of Dryer Road, between Cork Road and Malone Road. N42º 58.375 - W77º 26.416 The trail begins straight back (S) from the parking area, under a large oak tree.
Hiking Time:	1.5 hours one way
Length:	2.5 miles, one way (darkened trail)
Difficulty:	🥾 🥾 🥾
Surface:	Woods paths and mowed-grass paths
Trail Markings:	The connector trail has blue markers
Uses:	🚶 🎿 Trails within Dryer Road Park: 🚴
Dogs:	OK on leash
Admission:	Free

Contact:	Town of Victor, Parks & Recreation
	85 East Main Street, Victor, NY 14564-1397
	www.victorny.org/parks

One of the Town of Victor's newest parks, Dryer Road Park offers a playground, soccer fields, a skating rink, restrooms, and a network of mountain biking trails. Best of all, it connects to Ganondagan State Historic Site and has a particularly scenic hiking trail with a view of downtown Rochester in the distance. Between Dryer Road Park and Fort Hill, the trail traverses the top of a plateau ridge. The side loops follow the perimeter of fields on top of the plateau, then drop down off the plateau.

Trail Directions

- From the Ganondagan parking area head north through the opening in the split-rail fence to cross a mowed-grass area toward a sign "Trail of Peace."
- Pass the longhouse. Head into the woods behind it, passing the silver and black "Ethnobotanical Trail" sign.
- Pass the red trail junction, then continue straight through the next junction, leaving the purple trail.
- Continue heading west to cross Great Brook and School Street.
- Follow the blue trail back uphill to the Fort Hill plateau.
- On top of Fort Hill, turn right, still following blue blazes and head into the woods.
- The blue trail will lead to the parking area in Dryer Road Park.

Date Hiked: _____

Notes:

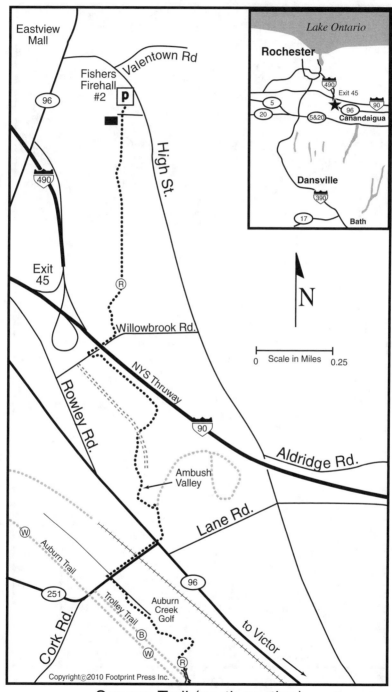

Seneca Trail (north section)

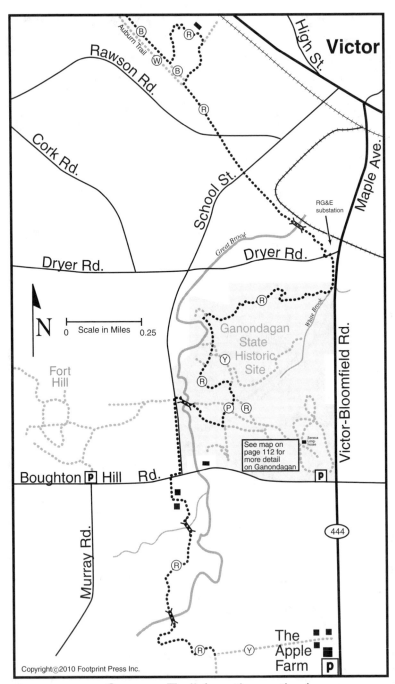

The Apple Farm

Seneca Trail (south section)

28

Seneca Trail

Location:	Victor, Ontario County
Directions:	From New York State Thruway exit 45, head south on Route 96. In Victor, turn south on Maple Avenue (State Route 444). Pass Boughton Hill Road then watch to the right for the Apple Farm (16410 State Route 444). (Hiking opens at 9:30 AM during fall hunting season.)

Alternative Parking: From Route 444, turn west on Boughton Hill Road (County Road 41). The parking area for Ganondagan State Historic Site is on Boughton Hill Road, near the corner of Victor-Bloomfield Road (State Route 444). N42° 57.685 - W77° 24.788

Alternative Parking: Fishers Firehall on the south side of High Street, Victor (0.25 mile south of Valentown Museum). N43° 1.225 - W77° 25.994

Hiking Time:	4.5 hours one way
Length:	7.8 miles one way
Difficulty:	👣 👣 👣
Surface:	Mowed-grass and dirt trail
Trail Markings:	Yellow, purple, and red blazes and diamond-shaped, red metal markers, yellow Victor Hiking Trails markers
Uses:	🚶
Dogs:	OK
Contact:	Victor Hiking Trails
	85 East Main Street, Victor, NY 14564-1397
	(585) 234-8226 message line
	www.victorhikingtrails.org

This trail is steeped in history and is a wonder of diverse terrain. The journey begins at the Apple Farm, then winds through Ganondagan State Historic Site, once the home of a thriving seventeenth-century Seneca Indian village. Its downfall came in 1687 when the Marquis de Denonville, Governor General of New France, led an army of 3,000 men from Canada to massacre the Seneca in an effort to eliminate them as competitors in the international fur trade business.

In 1998 a replica Seneca bark longhouse was built on the site using red cedar, white cedar, and hickory. It was built with intimate attention to detail using information from oral, archaeological, and historical records. The interior is furnished with hundreds of reproduced Seneca and European artifacts from 300 years ago to help interpret the history of the fur trade in the late 1600s and the relationship between the Seneca and the European colonists. The village at Ganondagan is thought to have had more than 150 longhouses, housing as many as 4,500 people. Each longhouse housed up to 20 families. Hours that the longhouse is open for viewing vary throughout the year. Call (585) 924-5848 for the current schedule.

From Ganondagan, this trail winds through Victor, passing through Ambush Valley. In 1687 when the Marquis de Denonville and his soldiers came to Ganondagan, most of the Seneca warriors were in Illinois fighting the French. The few who remained attempted to ambush Denonville's army in this narrow valley, but they were significantly outnumbered.

The Seneca Trail traverses wooded hills, crosses shrub fields, passes through wetlands, and follows two abandoned rail lines for part of its path. One was the Rochester and Auburn Railroad. The other was an electric trolley line that connected Rochester and Canandaigua before the advent of the interstate highway system. At one point along Seneca Trail, the hiker is treated to a view of the Rochester skyline in the distance.

Trail Directions
- From the Apple Farm parking lot, cross in front of the store then turn left before the yellow house and follow the gravel drive between the barns. (But, before heading out, stop in the store and stock up on apples, cider, pies, etc.)
- Continue straight, downhill, between orchards, on a mowed grass road.
- Yellow posts will verify that you're still on the trail.
- Turn right when the grass road meets a fence.
- At the "T," turn right and continue following yellow posts.
- Enter the woods.
- Head downhill and cross the creek on a bridge.
- The trail heads right, now marked with red VHT (Victor Hiking Trails) markers.
- Head uphill and follow the edge of the cliff just inside the woods. (Farm fields are to your left and the creek is below on the right.)
- Cross a tributary to the creek on a small bridge.
- Continue straight, passing several trails to the left.
- The trail winds left and heads between farm buildings.
- After the buildings, turn right onto the farm road.

- At 1.8 miles, cross Boughton Hill Road (County Road 41) and turn right.
- Turn left to follow School Street north.
- Watch for a double red blaze telling you to cross School Street and enter the woods at a green "State Park Lands" sign.
- Bear right at the "Y." (Left dead-ends at a creek without a bridge.)
- Cross a small bridge.
- Cross Great Brook on a longer bridge.
- At the "T," turn left, then bear right to continue away from the creek.
- At the next intersection, turn left onto the purple blazed trail.

A group on a guided hike sponsored by Victor Hiking Trails.

- Pass the red Sweetgrass Fork trail on the right.
- Cross plank boardwalks.
- Pass the yellow trail to the right (marked "to LH").
- Cross plank boardwalks.
- Continue following purple. (A small trail to the left dead-ends.)
- Pass the yellow trail to the right (again marked "to LH").
- Continue straight. The trail is now red blazed.
- At the next junction, bear right on the red-blazed Seneca Trail. (The purple trail bears left and ends at Great Brook.)
- Watch for a sharp right turn at the top of a bluff over the creek, marked by a yellow "Victor Hiking Trails" sign. Turn right to continue following the red trail.
- In a shrub field, bear right as a side trail heads to the left.
- Follow the red trail east to Victor-Bloomfield Road.
- Turn left along the road to cross a driveway, then head back into the woods.
- Turn left, cross Dryer Road, and head down the driveway of the RG&E substation.
- Go around the left side of the substation and turn left at the "Victor Hiking Trails" sign
- Cross the bridge over Great Brook and climb the hill.

- Pass a green gate.
- You are now on the abandoned Auburn rail line (red blazed).
- Cross School Street. This is now a segment of the Auburn Trail with its upgraded stone dust surface. Notice the marker denoting 84.5 miles from Syracuse.
- Cross Rawson Road.
- Watch for a right turn off the Auburn Trail, marked by a yellow "Victor Hiking Trails" sign. Turn right to follow the red-blazed Seneca Trail. It will loop past historic village artifacts (also known as a dump).
- Pass a blue trail (the Trolley Trail) to the left.
- The trail bends left.
- Turn left (W). (Straight leads to railroad tracks before Route 96).
- Pass abandoned metal and brick buildings on your right.
- Pass through a wetland area.
- Follow the red blazes through the woods.
- A right turn onto a straight segment of trail (marked orange to the left and red to the right) puts you on the abandoned trolley bed. (If leaves are off the trees, you can see the Auburn Trail running parallel to the left.)
- Pass a connector trail on the left. (It connects to the Auburn Trail.)
- The trail is now marked with blue markers.
- Cross a small wooden bridge.
- At the next junction, turn right and cross a wooden bridge. (Left connects to the Auburn Trail, straight is the continuation of the Trolley Trail.)
- Cross a boardwalk, then three wooden bridges.
- Emerge from the woods and cross a small wooden bridge.
- Turn left onto the driveway of Auburn Creek Golf.
- At Route 251, turn right and follow the road (no blazes along the road).
- Cross Route 96 at the crosswalk and turn left.
- Turn right and head uphill past the chain gate.
- Follow the old dirt road uphill. It will turn to grass.
- Part way up the hill, turn left (NW) off the road at the white arrow. Cross a small stream.
- Pass through conglomerate rocks, cross a farm road, and continue straight through a field, then through a shrub area.
- Bear left (another trail heads right) and descend into Ambush Valley (lined with horsetail plants). Watch for poison ivy.
- Pass a trail to the left that leads to a quarry area.
- Cross a gravel road and enter woods.
- Emerge from the woods and turn right through a field with great panoramic views to the left.
- Turn left (N) parallel to the Thruway and descend the hill.

- Cross a stone-lined creekbed.
- At Willowbrook Road, climb over the guardrail and turn right (E) to walk through two road tunnels under the New York State Thruway.
- After the metal gates on the left, turn left at the green and yellow "Hiking Trail" sign and climb the hill.
- Follow the red blazes on the wide, mowed path.
- Climb a long, gradual hill to a view of the Rochester skyline.
- Then a long downhill along the edge of the woods.
- Continue straight through a junction.
- Head uphill and turn right along the edge of a yard.
- At the gravel road, turn right, then cross grass to the firehall parking lot.

Date Hiked: _____

Notes:

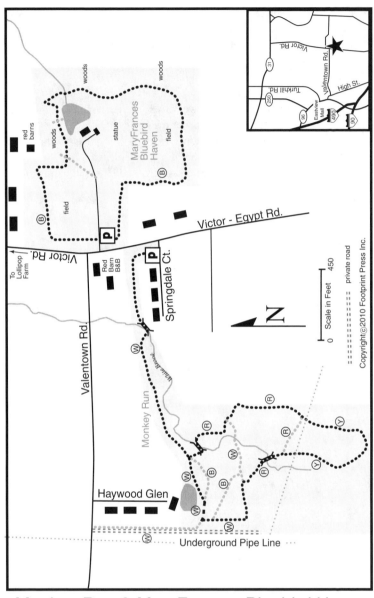

Monkey Run & MaryFrances Bluebird Haven

29

Monkey Run Trail

Location:	At the corner of Victor Egypt Road (County Road 9) and Springdale Court, Victor, Ontario County
Directions:	From Route 96, near Eastview Mall, turn east onto High Street and left (E) onto Valentown Road. Turn right (S) onto Victor - Egypt Road, and take the next right onto Springdale Court. Immediately turn right into the gravel parking area toward the yellow and green "Hiking Trail" sign. N43° 1.555 - W77° 24.022
Hiking Time:	45 minute loop
Length:	0.8-mile loop
Difficulty:	🥾 🥾 🥾 🥾
Surface:	Woodland path
Trail Markings:	Paint blazes, diamond metal & round plastic markers
Uses:	🚶 🎿
Dogs:	OK
Contact:	Victor Hiking Trails 85 East Main Street, Victor, NY 14564-1397 (585) 234-8226 message line www.victorhikingtrails.org

Valentown Road was formerly known as Monkey Run. The winding road reminded residents of a jungle vine wrapping around one tree after another, possibly providing a means of transport for an imaginary troupe of monkeys. The pond that the trail passes was known as the Black Lagoon by this property's former owners. It's home to snapping turtles.

A series of trail loops wind through the valley and hillsides of White Brook through a mature forest. White Brook is a twisting little waterway that adds a scenic dimension to this hike. The trails can be wet and muddy in early spring, but recent scout projects help keep your feet dry by providing bridges for the many brook crossings. Troop 86 scouts built 2 of the bridges. Nature signs along the way describe trees and vegetation that you pass. They were an Eagle Scout project of Zachary Rheaume from Troop 92.

Follow the trail markers to stay on the publically permissible trails. There are several side trails that lead to private homes.

Trail Directions
- From the Springdale Court parking area, go straight on the mowed path, past the yellow and green "Hiking Trail" sign. Head toward the left corner of the mowed area.
- Walk behind the houses on the mowed grass (no blazes) and head towards the woods.
- Enter the woods and pass a small side trail on the right.
- Cross White Brook on a wooden bridge. Follow the white "Victor Hiking Trails" logo signs.
- Pass a side trail on the left heading to homes.
- Pass a second side trail to homes.
- Come to a 4-way intersection. (Straight is the blue trail, left is the white trail and right isn't marked but should be white.) Turn Right.
- Pass a blue trail on the left.
- Pass a pond on the right. Exit the woods and turn left. (Note: the gravel road ahead leads to Valentown Rd.)
- Walk along the edge of the woods, heading south.
- Pass a blue trail on the left.
- The trail turns left into the woods.
- At the "Y," bear right on the red trail.
- Cross White Brook on a wooden bridge.
- At the "Y," bear right, following the yellow blazes.
- Exit the woods and cross an underground pipeline. Reenter the woods.
- Exit the woods and recross the pipeline. Pass the red trail on the left.
- Continue straight. The trail is now blazed red.
- Pass two side trails to the right heading to homes.
- Pass a white trail on the left.
- The red trail bears left, heading downhill.
- Cross White Brook on a culvert pipe.
- At the 4-way intersection, turn right and follow the white trail.
- Cross White Brook and follow the white trail back to the parking lot.

Date Hiked: _____
Notes:

30

MaryFrances Bluebird Haven

Location:	235 Victor Egypt Road (County Road 9), Victor, Ontario County (see the map on page 126)
Directions:	From Route 96, near Eastview Mall, turn east onto High Street and left (E) onto Valentown Road. Turn right (S) onto Victor Egypt Road and pull into driveway #235 near the large green "Welcome to MaryFrances Bluebird Haven" sign. The parking area is to the right. N43° 1.629 - W77° 23.996
Hiking Time:	30 minute loop
Length:	1.1-mile loop
Difficulty:	👣 👣 👣
Surface:	Mowed meadow and woodland path
Trail Markings:	Blue blazes on wooden stakes and trees, and blue VHT markers
Uses:	
Dogs:	Pets are NOT allowed
Contact:	Victor Hiking Trails 85 East Main Street, Victor, NY 14564-1397 (585) 234-8226 message line www.victorhikingtrails.org
	Town of Victor, Parks & Recreation 85 East Main Street, Victor, NY 14564-1397 www.victorny.org/parks

Welcome to the nature preserve known as the MaryFrances Bluebird Haven. This land was donated to the town of Victor in November 1996 for use as a bluebird sanctuary, by Robert Butler in memory of his wife, MaryFrances. An angel statue was added to the property at its dedication in June 1997. Watch for it as you hike. The Butler's bright blue house on the property is now used as a resource center by the Town of Victor.

The trail circumnavigates the property on a mowed path through a meadow and forest. Please follow the blue markers carefully and stay on the trail. Enjoy a quiet stroll on this forever-wild land without disturbing the nest boxes in the meadow areas. On a December afternoon hike we flushed a hawk and an owl from their perches as we hiked this trail.

Eastern bluebirds are in danger because they are cavity-nesting birds. The dead trees and wooden fence posts that once provided homes are rapidly disappearing as we convert our forests and farmlands to housing developments. Other species such as house sparrows and starlings compete with the bluebirds for the few remaining cavities. In many areas of the country, bluebird trails are being created to encourage bluebird survival. These consist of nesting boxes spaced at least 100 yards apart in fields and mowed-grass areas.

The MaryFrances Bluebird Haven is a bluebird habitat developed in support of the bluebird survival effort. This site has become an active breeding site for bluebirds and a living classroom, with an emphasis on preservation and restoration of New York's official state bird. For more information on bluebirds, visit the North American Bluebird Society web site at www.nabluebirdsociety.org.

Trail Directions
- From the parking area, head north on the mowed path, toward the "Trail Head" sign.
- Follow the well-marked blue trail around the perimeter of the field, then into the woods and back to field, to loop back to the parking area.

Date Hiked: _____

Notes:

Powder Mills Park

Set in steep, wooded hills, Powder Mills Park offers downhill skiing in the winter and fishing in Irondequoit Creek in the summer. The fish hatchery is also a favorite summer time attraction.

Development of the area began in 1850 when Daniel C. Rand arrived from Middletown, CT, where he worked as a manufacturer of blasting powder.

Rand came to this area and chose a small, ideal spot, far enough from settlements, but still close to the Erie Canal. In 1852 Rand opened his mill for making blasting powder in partnership with Mortimer Wadhams, and called it the Rand & Wadhams Powder Company.

The process for making blasting powder, which is simply a course version of gun powder, had been known for 100 years and involves grinding and mixing saltpeter (potassium nitrate), sulfur, and charcoal. To be an effective explosive, the ingredients have to be ground to an extremely fine consistency.

Irondequoit Creek was dammed to create a pond and a millrace for power to turn the great grinding stones and other machines used to pulverize the ingredients of blasting power. But it was a dangerous job. While in Connecticut, Rand had witnessed several accidents and his attention was drawn to the Rochester area by news of explosions that destroyed some powder mills in Allens Creek.

During construction of his new mill, Rand took several measures to help prevent or lessen the consequences of possible explosions. First, each step of the process was performed in a separate building so an explosion in one would not send the whole business up in flames. Rand also sought to eliminate sparks caused by metal touching metal. The buildings were connected by a narrow-gage railroad with wooden rails on which rode small cars with wooden wheels. And employees were not allowed to have any metal in their clothing. Many men even wore felt-soled slippers because their regular boots were constructed with nails.

Finally, to lessen the chance of fires or vandalism, Rand kept the property off limits to all hunting, fishing, and camping. This created the air of mystery about the area that lingered years after the mills were gone. In the 58 years of operation, several small explosions and two injuries occurred at the mill, but no catastrophic explosions or deaths.

Rand bought saltpeter and sulfur, but made his own charcoal out of willow trees that grew abundantly in the valley. Over the years Rand planted hundreds of new willows to replace those he cut. The willow was burned very slowly to produce charcoal. The charcoal and sulfur were ground together, with the saltpeter being ground separately. After both were reduced to course grain, they were combined and ground together for several hours. They were then formed into large cakes under 3,000 to 4,000 pounds of pressure. The cakes in turn were re-ground with graphite, which made the powder flow better. The powder was then sieved to different grades and packed in 25-pound kegs, with the finest being the most powerful blasting powder.

Rand died in 1883, and his partner passed on 3 years later. Rand's two sons, Mortimer and Samuel, continued the mill operation under the name D.C. Rand

Powder Company. The brothers quit the business in 1910 and moved to Uniontown, PA, to set up another mill closer to the coal mines that consumed the powder.

The property and buildings were left vacant until 1929 when 290 acres were purchased by the Monroe County Parks Commission. At that time the mill and homestead were razed.

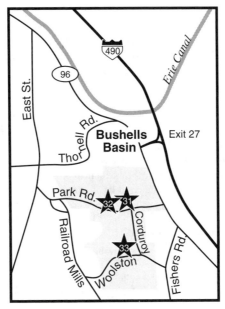

31- Daffodil Trail
32- Irondequoit Creek Trail
33- Fish Hatchery Trail

Trails in Powder Mills Park

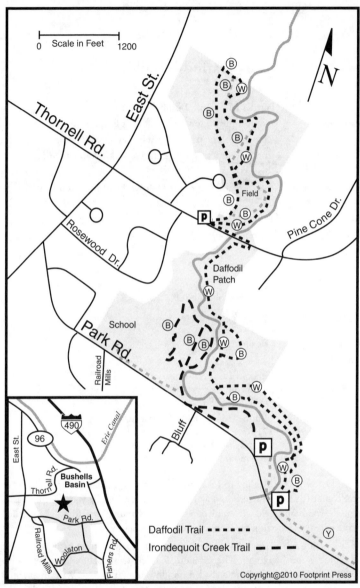

Daffodil Trail ·····
Irondequoit Creek Trail ─ ─ ─

Copyright©2010 Footprint Press

Daffodil Trail & Irondequoit Creek Trail

31

Daffodil Trail

Location:	Powder Mills Park, Bushnells Basin
Directions:	From Route 96 south of Bushnells Basin, turn west on Park Road. The parking area is on the east side of Irondequoit Creek where the creek flows under Park Road.
Alternate Parking:	A 4-car parking area on Thornell Road near Irondequoit Creek.
Hiking Time:	1.5 hours
Length:	3.4 mile loop
Difficulty:	
Surface:	Dirt path
Trail Markings:	White and blue blazes
Uses:	
Dogs:	OK on leash
Admission:	Free
Contact:	Pittsford Parks & Recreation
	35 Lincoln Avenue, Pittsford, NY 14534
	(585) 248-6280
	Monroe County Parks Department
	171 Reservoir Avenue, Rochester, NY 14620
	(585) 256-4950
	www.monroecounty.gov/parks-index.php

The Daffodil Trail is a joy to hike any time of year. It follows the contours of Irondequoit Creek as it winds its way through a valley. On the way the trail passes through woods and fields. It wanders near swamps and cliffs with houses perched on the edges, overlooking the Irondequoit Creek valley.

But by far, the best time of year to visit this trail is late April or early May when the daffodils are in bloom. The Pittsford Garden Club planted approximately 2,000 King Alfred daffodils in a shaded meadow along the trail. With the natural music from Irondequoit Creek flowing near, you can sit on a bench and soak in the beauty of a field of yellow blossoms.

You will be following a white-blazed trail on your way out and return on a combination of blue and white-blazed trails.

Trail Directions

- From the parking area, pass a yellow metal gate and follow white blazes through a mowed-grass area. (The blue-blazed trail labeled "Daffodil Meadow" will be part of your return loop.)
- Bear right at the wide grass area.
- Continue straight following white blazes at the next junction. (To the right is a blue trail, a #37 sign, and a dilapidated wooden bridge.)
- Bear right at the junction of the blue trail to keep following white.
- Pass another blue trail to the left, and continue straight, still following the white blazes.
- Pass a blue trail on the right.
- At 0.7 mile, reach the daffodil meadow and a bench for rest and reflection.
- As you approach Thornell Road the trail will bend right and climb the hill to road level.
- At 1.0 mile, cross Thornell Road, turn left, and walk along the shoulder of the road across the Irondequoit Creek bridge. (You may be tempted to use the paved walkway on the south side of Thornell Road but crossing Thornell Road further west puts you just below the crest of a hill. Cars appear rapidly and make crossing more dangerous.)
- When the guardrail ends, turn right and head downhill on a dirt path.
- Bear right on a smaller trail to stay on the white-blazed trail toward the bottom of the hill.
- Follow the bank of Irondequoit Creek.
- Stay on the small trail along the creek. (Blazes disappear.) (Ignore the wider mowed trail to your left.)
- At a "T," turn right.
- At the next intersection, turn right, heading back into woods.
- Continue following the creek and white blazes.
- At 1.6 miles reach a "T" and turn right onto the wide, mowed path. The creek is still on your right.
- Pass a trail to the left, and a mowed, white-blazed trail to the right that leads to the creek.
- A white-blazed trail merges from the left. Continue on the wide, mowed swath.
- Pass a white trail to the right.
- At the "T," turn left. (The trail to the right is white although the first visible blaze is blue.)
- At the "T," turn left.
- Pass a trail to the right.
- Go straight through multiple trail junctions (Right leads to Sugarwood Dr., left is a wide path, and a sharp left is a white trail.)
- Pass a wide trail on the left. Continue straight, uphill.
- Climb the hill to Thornell Road.
- At 2.4 miles, turn left (E) and follow the shoulder of Thornell Road to the end of the guardrail.
- Cross Thornell Road and head downhill to the creek.
- Bear left and follow white blazes.
- At 2.7 miles, pass through Daffodil Meadow.

The daffodils bloom in late March.

- Watch for blue blazes and turn left (E) at 2.8 miles.
- At a "T," turn left returning to the white-blazed trail.
- At a "Y," bear right on blue again.
- At a "T," turn right onto white.
- Just past the old wooden bridge, turn left onto the blue trail at #37.
- Follow this blue trail back to the parking area.

Date Hiked: _____

Notes:

Irondequoit Creek Trail

Location:	Powder Mills Park, Bushnells Basin
Directions:	From Route 96 south of Bushnells Basin, turn west on Park Road. The "West Area" parking area is on the west side of Irondequoit Creek where the creek flows under Park Road.
Alternate Parking:	None
Hiking Time:	30 minutes
Length:	1.1 mile loop
Difficulty:	
Surface:	Dirt path & mowed grass path
Trail Markings:	Blue markers
Uses:	
Dogs:	OK on leash
Admission:	Free
Contact:	Monroe County Parks Department
	171 Reservoir Avenue, Rochester, NY 14620
	(585) 256-4950
	www.monroecounty.gov/parks-index.php

The Irondequoit Creek Trail follows the southern shore of Irondequoit Creek then wanders in a loop through a forest in the Irondequoit Creek valley. Watch for ducks floating in Irondequoit Creek and deer bounding through the woods.

Trail Directions

- From the "West Area" parking area cross the mowed-grass area with Irondequoit Creek on your right and the West Shelter on your left.
- Enter the woods near the creek on a mowed grass trail at the "Easiest" ski sign and follow blue markers.
- The trail will follows the creek, then swings near Park Road.
- At a "T," turn right.
- Turn right again to stay near the creek.
- At the next "T," turn right to stay near the creek.
- Cross a narrow field (watch for birds), then come close to the creek again.
- Pass a trail to the left.
- At 0.6 miles be alert for the double blazes which tell you the trail doubles back, away from the creek.
- Pass a rusted old plow and disc beside the trail. To your left is a steep hill.
- Follow the blue blazes carefully as they snake through the woods.

- At 0.8 mile emerge to a mowed-grass field.
- Turn right at the junction.
- Bear left near the road.
- Continue straight, passing the trail you came out on, on the left. (The road is on your right.)
- Climb a small hill and continue straight to the parking area.

Date Hiked: _____

Notes:

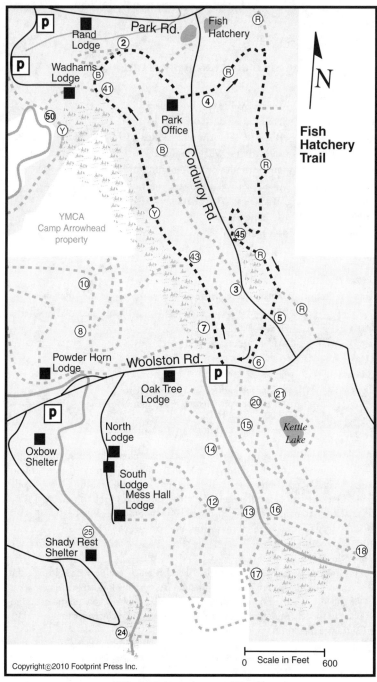

Fish Hatchery Trail

33

Fish Hatchery Trail

Location:	Powder Mills Park, Bushnells Basin
Directions:	From Interstate 490, exit at Bushnells Basin. Turn left on Route 96 (S), right on Park Road, left on Corduroy Road, and right on Woolston Road. Park in the gravel parking lot on the south side of Woolston Road before Oak Tree Shelter. (Not the paved parking lot next to the shelter.)
Alternative Parking:	Wadhams Lodge or at the fish hatchery
Hiking Time:	45 minutes
Length:	1.4 mile loop
Difficulty:	👣 👣 👣
Surface:	Dirt path
Trail Markings:	Small square plastic yellow markers, blue and white metal number signs on trees at trail junctions
Uses:	🚶 🎿
Dogs:	OK on leash
Admission:	Free
Contact:	Monroe County Parks Department 171 Reservoir Avenue, Rochester, NY 14620 (585) 256-4950 www.monroecounty.gov/parks-index.php

This trail begins along the edge of a swamp then climbs an esker. It then dips back down to cross Corduroy Road and climbs through a pine forest. Along the way, you have the option of taking two short side trails. One visits an old mill wheel. The other takes you to the fish hatchery. The fish hatchery is managed by the Riedman Foundation (www.fishpowdermill.org). In 2010 they released 17,000 brown trout into Powder Mills Park.

Trail Directions

- Cross Woolston Road. Pass through a wooden fence and bear right toward the woods until you see a trail. At this junction is a partially hidden junction marker #7 and the "Easiest" ski sign. (Behind the ski sign is a yellow plastic diamond blaze to the left.) Enter the woods and walk straight on the wider trail.
- Continue straight (N) past a trail to the left.
- Continue straight (N) past another trail that heads uphill to the right.
- At a wide junction, marked with a "More Difficult" ski sign, turn right (NE) and go uphill on the blue trail.

Brown trout grow in the Fish Hatchery pools.

Side Trip to Mill Wheel (0.1 mile): Continue straight (W) from the wide junction. Go past Wadhams Shelter and cross the creek. The mill wheel is in a fenced-in area on the right. Return to the wide junction.

- At the top of the hill continue straight. (To the left is a small side loop trail to a viewpoint at the top of an esker.)
- At 0.5 mile, continue straight (E) through junction marker #2. (The blue trail turns right here.)

    Side Trip to Fish Hatchery: Near the bottom of the hill is a trail to the left leading downhill, across a bridge, then across the road to the fish hatchery.

- Proceed to the parking lot of the park office building. Turn left and exit the parking lot.
- At 0.7 mile, cross Corduroy Road and proceed straight ahead across the mowed grass to junction marker #4 and a "Most Difficult" ski sign.
- Enter the woods and start uphill through a pine forest on the red trail.
- Reach a "T" at 0.8 mile (red in both directions) and turn right, uphill (S). The trail now weaves through the woods.
- Pass a side trail to the left.
- Watch for an extreme sharp turn as you head downhill at 1.1 miles.
- The trail levels out at the base of the hill and meets Corduroy Road at junction #45. Bear left continuing on the red trail. A wetland will be on your right.
- At the junction of an unmarked trail, turn right (W). Note: Watch carefully as the red trail bends left. You want to say straight on the unmarked trail. (If you reach

Woolston Road, you missed the turn off.)

• At junction marker #5 cross Corduroy Road and turn right (NW).

• After 30 feet reenter the woods on the left. This unmarked trail junction can be hard to see.

• At Woolston Road turn right (W) and follow the road back to the parking lot.

Volunteers gather brown trout for release at the Fish Hatchery.

Date Hiked: _____

Notes:

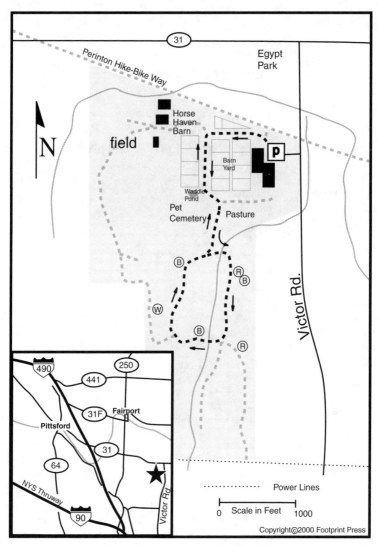

Lollypop Farm Trail

34

Lollypop Farm Trail

Location:	The Humane Society at Lollypop Farm, Fairport
Directions:	From Interstate 490, head east on Route 31. Turn right (S) on Victor Road and right (W) into the Lollypop Farm parking lot.
Alternative Parking:	None
Hiking Time:	45 minutes
Length:	1.3 mile loop
Difficulty:	👣 👣 👣
Surface:	Gravel, mowed-grass, and dirt paths
Trail Markings:	Within the woods, trails have red and blue paint bands around trees
Uses:	🚶 🎿
Dogs:	OK on leash
Admission:	Free
Contact:	Humane Society at Lollypop Farm PO Box 299, 99 Victor Road Fairport, NY 14450 (585) 223-1330 http://www.lollypop.org

Lollypop Farm is the home of the Humane Society of Monroe County. In 1999 it completed a major expansion and moved into new buildings to house stray and abandoned cats and dogs. The main building for animal viewing and adoption is open Monday through Saturday 10 AM to 8 PM and Sundays from 10 AM to 5 PM. The hours may change so call ahead for the latest information.

The trails are open every day from dawn to dusk. From the parking lot you'll walk down a gravel road, passing pens that house horses, fallow deer, ostriches, pigs, llamas, ducks, geese, and an ever changing variety of other animals. After crossing the pet cemetery, you'll enter the woods and complete a shaded loop through the hills in a mixed wood forest.

Trail Directions
- Head to the northwest corner of the parking lot and follow the gravel road, heading away from the main Lollypop Farm building.
- Pass a trail to the right which leads to the Perinton Hike-Bike Way (see details in *Take Your Bike! Family Rides in the Rochester Area*).
- Continue on the gravel road, between animal pastures.

- At the "T," turn left (S) and continue passing animal pastures.
- After Waddle Pond, the split-rail fence will end. Turn right (SE) and cross in front of the pet cemetery, heading toward another split-rail fence around a horse pasture.
- Follow the horse pasture split-rail fence toward the woods.
- At 0.3 mile, enter the woods on a mowed-grass path. The trail will be marked with red and blue paint bands on the trees.
- At 0.4 mile, turn left (E). (Straight will be part of the return loop.)
- Cross a small log bridge then the trail turns right (S).
- At 0.6 mile, cross another small log bridge.
- Reach an intersection at 0.6 mile. Turn right to head downhill. (The trail now has blue bands on the trees.)
- Head uphill into a pine woods.
- At the top of the hill proceed straight (N), heading downhill. (A hard-to-see trail heads left. It's a white-blazed trail that is passable but not maintained.)
- At 0.9 mile, pass a trail to the right. Continue straight.
- Cross back in front of the pet cemetery and reach the gravel road at 1.1 miles.
- Turn left and follow the gravel road past Waddle Pond and the other animal pens.
- At the trail intersection, turn right (E), passing additional pens.
- Pass the trail to the Perinton Hike-Bike Way on the left and continue to the parking lot.

Date Hiked: _____

Notes:

Trail Town USA and the
Crescent Trail Association

In 1996, Perinton was named one of the top 10 "Trail Towns" in the United States by the American Hiking Association. The Association recognizes communities that use trails to provide exercise for the body, stimulation of the mind and senses, and a personal connection with the community's natural beauty and past history. The forty miles of trails at the time, included the Crescent Trail, the Erie Canal Heritage Trail (also called the Erie Canalway Trail), and the Perinton Hike-Bike Way, achieved this goal within Perinton. Since then, the trail network has continued to grow.

The Crescent Trail Association is a volunteer organization which was organized in 1980 to develop, promote, and maintain public hiking trails in the Town of Perinton. The name originated from the concept of a long, diagonal trail through the town. When viewed on a map, it resembled a crescent moon. Currently, they have over 35 miles of trails passing through woods, marshland, and meadows. The trails converge into the Erie Canal Heritage Trail and an old trolley-bed trail, the Perinton Hike-Bike Way.

Many individual landowners have granted permission for trails to cross their property. The continued use of the trails and the opening of additional sections depend upon hikers respecting the rights of landowners.

– Obey posted signs and respect landowners rights

– No bicycles or motorized vehicles

– No littering, dumping, fires, or camping

– Please protect trees, plants, and crops

– Stay on the trail and hike at your own risk

The Crescent Trail Association welcomes new members. They sponsor a guided hike along a portion of their trails on the second Sunday of each month. Hikes are open to the public. To hear the latest schedule call (585) 234-1621 or check web site www.perinton.org/Departments/RandP/hikingctha. Two beautiful full-color maps of the extensive network of trails in Perinton are available for $1 each at the Perinton Town Hall & Community Center, 1350 Turk Hill Road, Fairport.

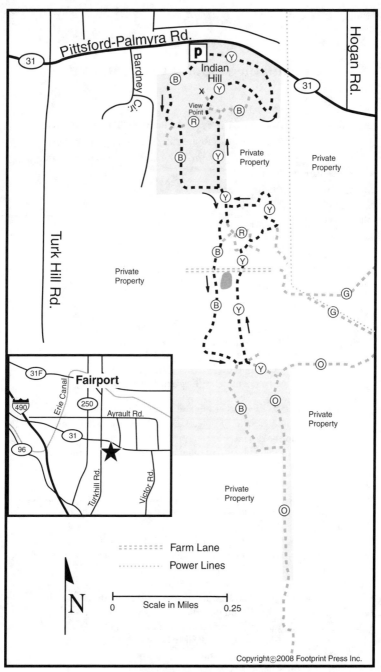

Pittsford-Palmyra Rd.

31

Hogan Rd.

P

Indian Hill

31

B

X

Y

View Point

Y

B

R

Turk Hill Rd.

B

Y

Private Property

Private Property

Y

Y

R

Private Property

B

Y

G

B

G

Y

Private Property

O

Y

O

Private Property

B

O

Private Property

O

31F

Fairport

Erie Canal

490

250

Ayrault Rd.

31

96

★

Turkhill Rd.

Victor Rd.

Farm Lane

Power Lines

N

0   Scale in Miles   0.25

Indian Hill Section

147

35

Indian Hill Section - Crescent Trail

Location:	Route 31, Perinton
Directions:	From Interstate 490, take Route 31 (Pittsford-Palmyra Road) east. Pass Route 250. The parking area will be on the right between Turk Hill Road and Hogan Road.
Alternative Parking:	None
Hiking Time:	1 hour
Length:	2.1 mile loop
Difficulty:	🦶 🦶 🦶
Surface:	Dirt and mowed-field paths
Trail Markings:	Orange and blue blazes painted on trees
Uses:	🚶
Dogs:	OK
Admission:	Free
Contact:	The Crescent Trail Association, Inc.
	P.O. Box 1354, Fairport, NY 14450
	(585) 234-1621
	www.perinton.org/Departments/RandP/hikingctha/

This trail is well-blazed and easy-to-follow. It goes through meadows and woods to a high vantage point (elevation 714 feet) overlooking suburban Perinton and the Rochester skyline in the distance. In the rear (S) section you'll see farm fields and horse pastures. Follow blue blazes outbound and yellow blazes for the return.

Trail Directions

- From the parking area, head through the split-rail fence, straight (S), uphill. (At the start of the trail you'll pass a trail to the left which will be part of the return loop.)
- At the Y, bear left. (The trail to the right dead-ends at a field.)
- At the clearing, turn right to stay on the blue-blazed trail. (Left is a trail up to the viewpoint.)
- Pass through the woods and cross a field heading south.
- Reach the edge of the field at 0.3 mile. Turn left (E) along the edge of the field.
- At a junction turn right (SE) on the yellow trail. (Watch for poison ivy.)
- Pass a yellow trail to the left. Continue straight on the blue trail.
- Head into a gully and cross a brook. Bear right on the blue trail. (To the left is an unblazed trail.)
- The blue trail makes a big S curve out of the gully.

- At 0.6 mile, pass the red trail to the left. Continue straight (S) inside the woods on the blue trail.
- Cross wood planks.
- Cross a gravel farm road at 0.6 mile, and continue straight (S) on the blue trail, past a pond on your left. The view is of farm fields & horse pastures.
- Continue straight as the blue trail turns right (S).
- Reach a junction with yellow to the left and right. Straight is an unmarked trail that goes to an open field. Turn left (N) onto yellow.
- Pass the pond again on the left.
- Cross the farm road, staying on the yellow trail. A Porta Potty is in the bushes.
- Cross a gully on a small bridge.
- At the "T," turn right, staying on yellow. (Left is an unmarked trail.)
- Pass a small, unmarked side trail on the right. (It leads to the open field).
- Turn right at double yellow blaze and cross the creek on a small bridge. (Straight ahead is the red trail.)
- Pass unmarked trail on left (a cut over from red trail).
- The yellow trail takes a hard left. (A small unlabeled trail heads toward the power lines.)
- Cross creek on bridge
- Cross a wet area on planks.
- At a T, turn right, continuing on yellow (N). (Watch for poison ivy.)
- Bear right and cross the field heading north.
- Leave the field and enter woods. Bear left on yellow to the viewpoint & picnic table area. (Blue goes straight.)
  (Note: a side trail heads east from the picnic table and connects to the blue trail.)
- Continue straight (N) across the field where trail "Y's". Bear right. (Left is an unmarked trail that is blocked off.)
- Pass the blue trail on the right, continuing straight.
- Head downhill and follow the yellow trail as it doubles back. Watch for poison ivy. Pine trees indicate you're almost back to the parking lot.

Date Hiked: _____
Notes:

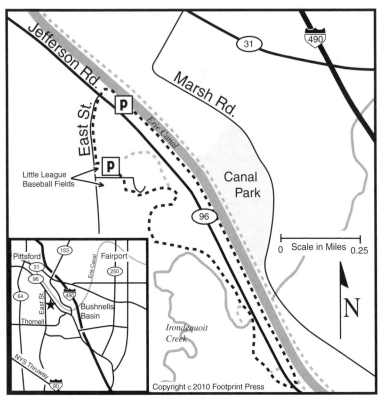

Copyright c 2010 Footprint Press

Cartersville - Great Embankment Loop Trail

36

Cartersville - Great Embankment Loop Trail

Location: Along the Erie Canal, Pittsford

Directions: Park in the Little League parking lot off East Street,
near the corner of Jefferson Road (Route 96)

Alternative Parking: Route 96 near East Street, next to the canal

Hiking Time: 1 hour and 15 minute loop

Length: 2.2 mile loop

Difficulty:

Surface: Mowed-grass and dirt

Trail Markings: White and blue blazes

Uses:

Dogs: OK on leash

Admission: Free

Contact: Pittsford Parks & Recreation
35 Lincoln Avenue, Pittsford, NY 14534
(585) 248-6280

The area you will walk is steeped in history. Once the site of Cartersville, a busy nineteenth century canal port, it had a distillery, warehouses, and a facility for changing the mules and horses that towed the canal boats.

You'll walk on top of the Great Embankment, one of the greatest achievements of the pioneer canal builders. Their challenge was to have the canal span the 70-foot-deep, one-mile-wide Irondequoit Creek Valley. They used earth from the local area to form mounds to join the natural glacial meltwater hills of the Cartersville esker to create embankments. The great embankment was originally built in 1821-22 and was enlarged several times. It remains today, the longest embankment on the Erie Canal.

Two guard gates, one just west of the trail and one just east of the Interstate 490 bridge at Bushnells Basin, isolate this section of canal in case of leaks or breaks in the embankment. This happened in 1974 when contractors tunneling under the embankment, inadvertently pierced the waterway. Forty homes were damaged or destroyed as the waters rushed downhill through a 100-foot hole in the bottom of the canal before the gates could be closed. As you cross the embankment, watch for a manhole cover next to the canal. This provides access to a ladder in a shaft leading to the base of the concrete embankment trough, allowing engineers to periodically check the embankment for leaks.

The section of Irondequoit Creek that you'll pass was once home to Simon Stone's gristmill and sawmill. Mr. Stone, a Revolutionary War veteran and founder of Pittsford, built his mills in the early 1790s. Milling in this area continued until 1913, when the canal enlargement displaced the mills.

In September 1998 history was once again made at this location. A derecho, or sudden, violent downdraft of air swept through ripping and uprooting the large trees. You'll see evidence littered on the forest floor as you walk this trail. Imagine the power of the derecho (commonly called a microburst) as you hike along.

A portion of the trail follows close to the edge of the Erie Canal. Watch small children carefully. Also be aware that poison ivy grows along this trail.

Trail Directions
- From the parking lot, head south over the grass toward the Pittsford Trails marker on a post.
- Follow the blazes around the outside perimeter of a former dump, now grass covered. (Woods will be to your right and a grass hill to your left.)
- Cross over a small culvert onto the dirt town maintenance road.
- At 0.2 mile, bear right (SE) to head downhill, still following the white blazes.
- A blue-blazed trail enters from the left. It is a shortcut back to the ball fields. Continue following the white-blazed path through the woods.
- At 0.6 mile, Irondequoit Creek appears on the right. Jefferson Road (Route 96) is above you on the left.
- A path veers off to the right. (For a short side venture follow this path down some steps to Irondequoit Creek. The culvert you'll be looking at takes the creek under Route 96 and the canal. It was built in 1916.)
- Continue straight (S) on the white-blazed trail. Wind through the woods.
- Toward the top of a steep hill (at 0.9 mile) is a yellow metal barricade off Route 96. Bear right and continue uphill.
- When you reach Route 96 at 1.0 mile, turn left and cross very carefully. The trail from here follows the south side of the canal. Watch small children carefully. (A right turn connects to the orange-blazed Crescent Trail. The towpath (Erie Canalway Trail) is on the opposite side of the canal.)
- Turn left (N) and follow the mowed-grass path along the edge of the canal. (The canal along this section has high cement walls and banked sides. This is the highest point of the Great Embankment.)
- Pass a wooden rail fence and continue along the canal edge.
- At 1.2 miles, pass the metal "30" sign and the manhole covering the embankment shaft.
- At 1.7 miles, begin crossing through a gravel parking and picnic area between Route 96 and the canal.
- Cross Route 96 when you reach East Street at 1.9 miles.
- Follow East Street back to the Little league Baseball Fields parking lot.

Date Hiked: _____
Notes:

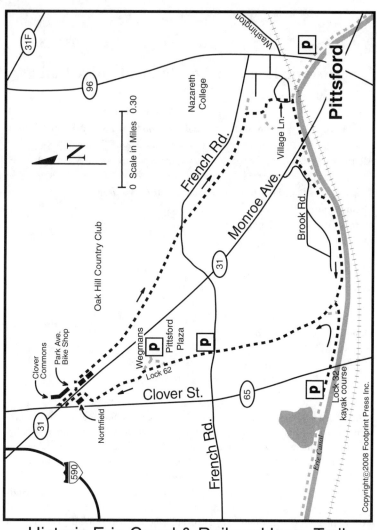

Historic Erie Canal & Railroad Loop Trail

37

Historic Erie Canal & Railroad Loop Trail

Location:	Lock #32 Canal Park, Route 65, Pittsford
Directions:	From Rochester, head south on Clover Street (Route 65). Just before the canal, turn west into Lock #32 Canal Park.
Alternative Parking:	At the back of the Wegmans parking lot on Monroe Avenue, Pittsford
	French Road, between Route 65 and Route 31.
Hiking Time:	3 hours
Length:	5.2 mile loop
Difficulty:	
Surface:	Mowed-grass, dirt, and paved paths
Trail Markings:	Pittsford Trails markers
Uses:	
Dogs:	OK on leash
Admission:	Free
Contact:	Pittsford Parks and Recreation
	35 Lincoln Avenue, Pittsford, NY 14534
	(585) 248-6280

As the name of the trail implies, you will be walking on not one, but two historic transportation paths. The original Erie Canal, known as "Clinton's Ditch," headed north to Rochester. It was opened in 1822, enlarged in the 1850s, and closed in 1920. Mules and horses pulled the canal boats on a towpath next to the canal. You'll walk on some of it, but the rest is now Interstates 590 and 490.

Along the way, you'll see evidence of the Odenbach Shipyard, which made landing crafts during World War II, and Lock 62 built in 1855 as part of the first canal expansion. Lock 62 was doubled in 1870 and lengthened in 1887, then abandoned in 1920 when the new canal was routed south of Rochester.

You'll pass Northfield Food & Drink, housed in a historic federal-style building that has been in use since its days as a canal inn starting in the 1830s. At its peak, this area included a resort and spa with a healing sulphur and mineral spring, an amusement pavilion, and bowling alleys. If you have limited time, we recommend the 1.7-mile section from Lock 32 to the Northfield and back, both for its scenic and historic qualities.

After crossing busy Route 31, you will continue your journey on the Rochester and Auburn rail bed, an active railroad from 1840 through 1960. It was the first railroad east of Rochester and became part of the New York Central system. Both of these sections are maintained by the Pittsford Parks Department. Development along Monroe Avenue in 1999 encroached on the trail. Access the trail by cutting through the parking area just east of Park Ave Bike. After a short section that skirts the back of businesses, the path returns to being a wooded railbed.

The third leg of the trip takes you along the present-day Erie Canal for a scenic walk back to Lock 32 Canal Park. Lock 32 was built in 1912 and still operates today. On the south side of the lock, a white water kayak course was built in 2001. It's worth walking across the Route 65 bridge to see if any boats are at play.

Trail Directions

- From the canal towpath adjacent to the parking area, head down a flight of steps that takes you beneath Route 65. Once you have reached the bottom, you will have a great view of the lock to your right.
- Continue straight (E) along the canal path.
- After 0.3 mile, the path will head slightly inland from the canal. After passing a small trail to your left, you will quickly arrive at a map post showing "Historic Erie Canal & Railroad Loop Trail." Turn left onto the mowed-grass path.
- As you walk, notice the remains of the old canal bed on your left.
- The trail continues for half a mile before widening into an old road. Shortly after this, at about 0.9 mile, you will see remains of the Odenbach Shipyard to your left through the trees and brush.
- Cross French Road and a trail parking area at 1 mile. The path narrows to 6 feet.
- The back of Pittsford Plaza emerges on your right.
- Just after an access trail to the plaza and Wegmans branches off to your right, you will arrive at Lock #62.
- Just past the lock, head down a flight of steps. Turn right, then bear left to cross a small bridge at 1.3 miles. Going straight at the base of the steps will bring you to the second lock.
- Turn right after the bridge. (Left leads to private homes.) You are now walking in the old canal bed.
- The trail brings you to the rear parking area adjacent to Northfield Food & Drink.
- From the parking area, go to the sidewalk along Monroe Avenue and turn left to reach the corner of Clover and Monroe.
- Cross Monroe Avenue. Turn right onto the sidewalk, then take a quick left to cut through the parking area just past (E) Park Ave Bike. Take a right on the dirt path that runs behind the strip of businesses.
- You are now traveling on the old Rochester and Auburn Railroad. The path travels over a sometimes rough path behind several businesses on Monroe Avenue.
- The trail returns to a wooded path. Oak Hill Country Club is to your left for much of this section.
- At 2.9 miles, cross French Road and continue along the railroad bed.
- A cement pillar with a "W" on it will be on your left at about 3.2 miles. It signaled the engineer to blow the train's whistle.
- Pass a cement battery box on the left at 3.5 miles.
- You will soon see a single-story red brick building ahead, on the left side of the path. BEFORE getting to this building, take the side trail that branches off to the right.

- At the "T," turn left and head in the direction of another red brick building.
- Turn right on the paved road and follow it to the canal towpath.
- Turn right (W) on the canal towpath.
- Walk under the Monroe Avenue bridge at 4 miles.

You will now take one of two paths, depending on what day and time you are hiking. During business hours (7AM-5PM, Mon-Fri) you will need to go around the NYS canal property. If you are hiking during "off hours" you can continue straight along the canal path.

Alternate Route (for business hours):
- Just after crossing under the bridge, take a right.
- Take a left at Brook Road.
- After passing the NYS canal property on your left, a path to the left heads slightly uphill to rejoin the canal path.

Canal Path (non-business hours):
- Continue straight along the canal path, passing the NYS canal property to your right. The trail bends right and the canal is not in view for a short period.
- A trail comes in from the right (see alternate route, above).

Both Routes:
- Follow the towpath, heading West.
- At 4.5 miles, the canal comes into view again.
- At 4.9 miles you will pass the marker for the "Historic Erie Canal and Railroad Loop" on your right, continue straight.
- Follow the canal path and go up the steps that lead to Lock 32 Canal Park.

Date Hiked: _____
Notes:

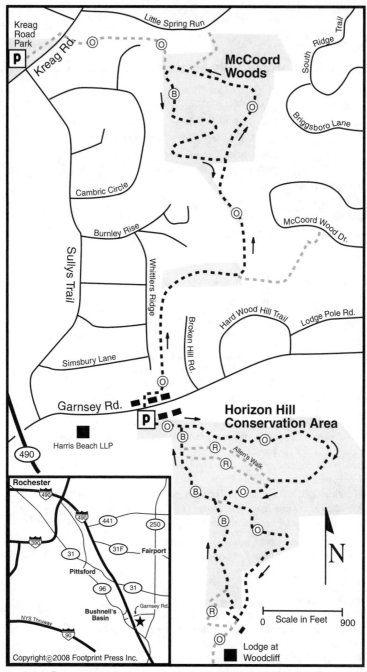

McCoord Woods & Horizon Hill Sections

38

McCoord Woods Section - Crescent Trail

Location:	Garnsey Road, Fairport
Directions:	Take the Bushnells Basin exit from Interstate 490. Turn left (S) on Route 96 and left on Garnsey Road. The parking area will be on the right shortly after Citibank.
Alternative Parking:	None
Hiking Time:	1.5 hours
Length:	2.8 mile loop
Difficulty:	👞 👞 👞 👞
Surface:	Dirt path
Trail Markings:	Orange and blue blazes painted on trees
Uses:	🚶
Dogs:	OK
Admission:	Free
Contact:	The Crescent Trail Association, Inc. P.O. Box 1354, Fairport, NY 14450 (585) 234-1621 www.perinton.org/Departments/RandP/hikingctha/

This well-blazed, easy-to-follow trail begins as a narrow stretch of land between the backyards of private homes but quickly turns to wilderness in terrain sculpted by glaciers. The derecho of September, 1998 felled trees and thinned some sections of this forest trail. According to meteorologist Kevin Williams, "a derecho is a fast-moving, long-lived storm that produces winds in excess of 58 miles per hour over a path at least 280 miles in length. The term was coined by Gustavus Hinrichs, director of the Iowa Weather Service about 1885. He made it up from a Spanish word for "straight ahead," because the debris field from a derecho tends to fall in the same direction."

For a quick escape from civilization and an aerobic workout, this trail can't be beat.

Trail Directions
- From the parking area, cross Garnsey Road at the marked crosswalk.
- Head north on the trail, between houses, passing the "Crescent Trail" sign with an orange marker.
- Turn right along a creek, then cross a bridge over the small creek.
- Follow the orange blazes through backyards.

- The trail turns left and enters the woods at 0.1 mile.
- Pass a neighborhood access trail to the left.
- At 0.4 mile, a small creek appears on your left.
- Turn left (E) on the orange trail, cross a bridge, then a raised boardwalk. (A white blaze trail continues straight.)
- Several small trails lead off; stay on the orange trail.
- Follow switchbacks up a steep hillside at 0.6 mile. Stay on the orange marked trail.
- Cross a small plank bridge.
- At 0.9 mile, turn right on the orange trail as it meets the blue trail.
- The trail heads uphill to the top of an esker. (Sorry, no view - except when leaves are off the trees.)
- Follow the orange trail down off the esker.
- Pass a small tree-trunk lined, steep, short-cut trail to the right.
- Stay on the orange trail as you pass the white trail to the right.
- At the blue trail junction leave orange and turn left (SW) on the blue trail. (The orange trail leads to Kreag Road Park.)
- Cross a plank bridge at 1.4 miles.
- At the orange trail junction turn right (SW) onto the orange trail.
- Cross a plank bridge.
- Head down the switchbacks. Stay on the orange trail.
- At 2.2 miles, pass an unmarked trail to the left. It leads to the white trail.
- Cross a raised boardwalk, then a small bridge over a creek.
- Turn right (NW) on the orange trail. (To the left is the white trail.)
- Pass a neighborhood access trail to the right.
- Reach the mowed-grass area at 2.7 miles. Turn right and follow the edge of the property until you cross a bridge.
- Turn left, then cross Garnsey Road to the parking area.

Date Hiked: _____
Notes:

39

Horizon Hill Section - Crescent Trail

Location:	Garnsey Road, Fairport
Directions:	Take the Bushnells Basin exit from Interstate 490. Turn left (S) on Route 96 and left on Garnsey Road. The parking area will be on the right shortly after Citibank.
Alternative Parking:	None
Hiking Time:	75 minutes
Length:	2.2 mile loop
Difficulty:	🦶 🦶 🦶 🦶
Surface:	Dirt path
Trail Markings:	Orange and blue blazes painted on trees
Uses:	🚶
Dogs:	OK
Admission:	Free
Contact:	The Crescent Trail Association, Inc. P.O. Box 1354, Fairport, NY 14450 (585) 234-1621 www.perinton.org/Departments/RandP/hikingctha/

Hilly terrain on this hike makes it great for a short, strenuous workout. The trail wanders through the glacially sculpted hills in the woods between Garnsey Road and Woodcliff Lodge giving a spectacular view of the Irondequoit Creek Valley and Rochester in the distance. On our last trip here, we watched a fox cross the grass south of the parking area.

There are many intersecting trails but the main trails are well marked with colored blazes. Watch carefully for double blazes which signal trail intersections or turns. The loop described follows the orange trail outbound and the blue trail returning.

You may want to use this trail to test your child's blaze-following abilities. Or, as a treat for yourself or your family, hike to Woodcliff Lodge for brunch, then hike back.

Trail Directions
- From the parking area head through a gap in the split-rail fence, walking east on the orange trail.
- Pass a white trail, then a blue trail to the right.
- Continue straight on the orange trail as it crosses a bridge and heads uphill.

One of the joys of hiking is finding a scene like this.
A mourning dove and her two babies rest on a rock beside the trail.

- Cross a small bridge, a short boardwalk, then another small bridge.
- At 0.5 mile, watch for the double orange blazes at the top of a climb. The orange trail turns right.
- Head downhill and walk parallel to a small creek.
- Turn left and cross a bridge. (Straight takes you to the red trail.)
- Another red trail heads to the right just after the bridge. Continue uphill.
- Continue following the orange trail as it turns several times at double blazes.
- At one double blaze a small connector trail leads left. Bear right and pass a bench in a clearing that affords a great view of downtown Rochester.
- After the bench, turn left, and continue on the orange trail. (Straight is a blue trail.)
- Bear left and stay on the orange trail as you climb another hill. (Another blue trail heads off to the right.)
- Pass the shortcut trail on the left.
- At 0.9 mile, watch for double blazes and turn right half way up a hill. (An unmarked trail continues straight.)
- Descend, then ascend again.
- The orange trail turns right and parallels Woodcliff Golf Course, still inside the woods.
- Small trails to the left lead to the Woodcliff Golf Course fairway.
- The trail bears right at the Woodcliff grounds-keeping area.
- Turn left at the double blaze. (The unmarked trail to the right heads downhill.)
- Shortly, watch for a small trail on the right. Turn right (W) on the blue trail and begin the return leg on the blue trail. (Or you can continue on the orange trail to the overlook behind Woodcliff Lodge for a wonderful view of the city. From here, you can cross the grass to Woodcliff Drive and continue following the orange trail as it winds around the Woodcliff subdivision.) (Another option is to bear right on the red trail loop and extend your hike 0.4 mile.)
- At 1.6 miles, follow the blue trail, turning right (E) at the double blaze.
- Follow blue blazes as the trail winds downhill.

- Cross a small bridge over a creek.
- Immediately after the bridge, turn left on a newly blazed blue trail. (The old faded blue blazed trail continues straight.)
- Turn left at a double blaze. (To the right is unmarked, but becomes the faded blue trail.)
- Pass a connector trail to the right.
- Follow the bright blue blazes as the trail turns. (Straight is the former blue trail which is no longer maintained through a field.)
- Emerge to a grass field and bear right along the woods' edge.
- Pass a trail to the right. (It is a red trail heading into the woods.)
- Pass a second red trail to the right. (This is Alan's Walk.)
- Pass a trail to the right. (It's a new white-blazed trail that connects to the orange trail.)
- Meet the orange trail and turn left to return to the parking area.

Date Hiked: _____

Notes:

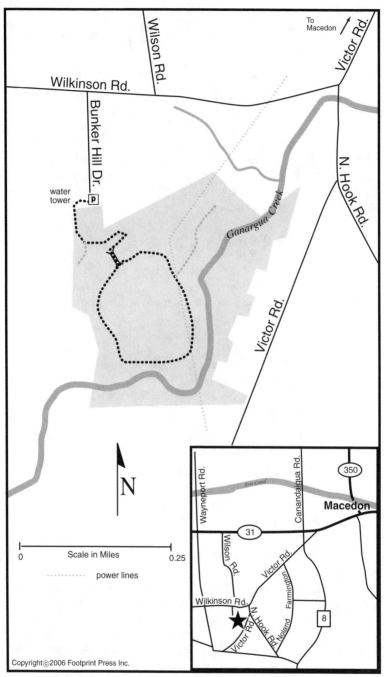

Ganargua Creek Meadow Preserve

40

Ganargua Creek Meadow Preserve

Location:	Bunker Hill Drive, Macedon, Wayne County
Directions:	From Route 31, west of Macedon, head south on Wayneport Road. Turn left (E) onto Wilkinson Road, then right (S) onto Bunker Hill Drive. Drive to the end of the road, and park in spaces on the left. N43° 2.480 - W77° 20.949
Hiking Time:	30 minute loop
Length:	1-mile loop
Difficulty:	👣 👣 👣 👣
Surface:	Dirt trail down hillside then mowed field trail through the meadow
Trail Markings:	Green and white metal markers along the woods trail, none in the meadow
Uses:	
Dogs:	OK on leash (please clean up after your pet)
Contact:	Genesee Land Trust 500 East Avenue, Suite 200, Rochester, NY 14607 (585) 256-2130 www.geneseelandtrust.org

The Ganargua Creek Meadow Preserve trail begins at the water tower, high on top of Bunker Hill. It winds down a steep hillside through an oak forest to the floodplain meadow of Ganargua Creek. Hemmed in by hills, a mowed path circles around the grassy meadow. Look for butterflies and evidence of the power of water in spring runoff as you hike the meadow, but keep an eye out for poison ivy. Go when the leaves are off the trees for the best view from Bunker Hill.

This land was donated to the Genesee Land Trust in 1996 for preservation in honor of Tim Johnson by his mother and step-father, Cynthia and Leo Kesselring. The trail was built by a class of RIT students in 2002 and is now maintained by the Macedon Trails Committee.

Trail Directions

- From the parking area, head up the hill toward the water tower. The trail begins to the left, in the woods. Follow it downhill.

- Cross the bridge at the base of the hill, and follow the perimeter trail around the meadow.
- Cross the bridge again, and head uphill to the parking area.

Date Hiked: _____

Notes:

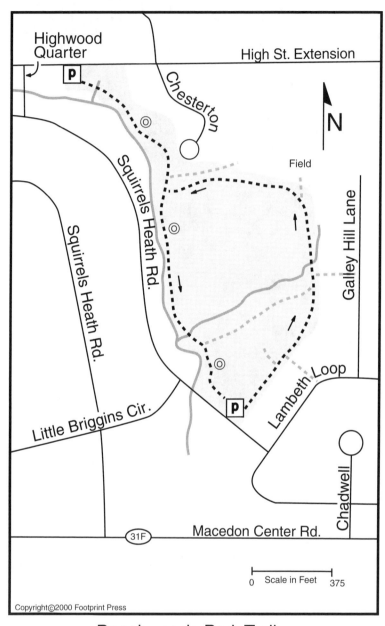

Highwood Quarter

High St. Extension

Chesterton

P

N

Field

Squirrels Heath Rd.

Galley Hill Lane

Squirrels Heath Rd.

P

Lambeth Loop

Little Briggins Cir.

Chadwell

31F

Macedon Center Rd.

0   Scale in Feet   375

Copyright©2000 Footprint Press

Beechwoods Park Trail

41

Beechwoods Park Trail

Location:	High Street Extension, Perinton
Directions:	From South Main Street, Fairport, head east on High Street. Continue past Turk Hill Road onto High Street Extension. The parking area for Beechwoods Park will be on the right, past Highwood Quarter.
Alternate Parking:	Southern end of the park on Squirrels Heath.
Hiking Time:	45 minutes
Length:	1.2 mile loop
Difficulty:	
Surface:	Dirt path
Trail Markings:	Orange blazes on trees along sections of trail
Uses:	
Dogs:	OK on leash
Admission:	Free
Contact:	Perinton Recreation & Parks Department 1350 Turk Hill Road, Fairport, NY 14450

Beechwoods Park is a 22.8-acre passive greenbelt through a residential area. It is forested with beech, birch, and maple trees. The northern section of trail is a narrow swath through the woods. The southern section has a wide, board-lined trail. The direct route from High Street Extension to Squirrels Heath is orange blazed. It was cleared and blazed by Boy Scout Troop 280. Much of the return loop is unblazed.

Trail Directions
- From the parking area on High Street Extension, head southeast on a gravel path.
- Cross a small wooden bridge.
- Cross a paved walkway and head into the woods.
- Bear left along the edge of a small stream.
- At 0.3 mile, pass a wooden bridge to the right and a trail intersection. Continue straight on the orange-blazed trail.
- Cross a stream bed. The trail will become wide and board-lined.
- Turn right (S) to continue following orange blazes.
- At 0.6 mile, at the parking area on Squirrels Heath, take a sharp left to head back into the woods on an unmarked trail.

- At 0.7 mile the boards lining the trail will end and a paved path will head right to Lambeth Loop. Turn left to follow the narrow woods trail.
- At the "T," turn right. (Left leads back to the orange-blazed trail.)
- Cross a stream bed.
- At a "Y," bear left. Head downhill until you meet the orange-blazed trail.
- Turn right (N) onto the orange-blazed trail and follow it back to the parking area.

Date Hiked: _____

Notes:

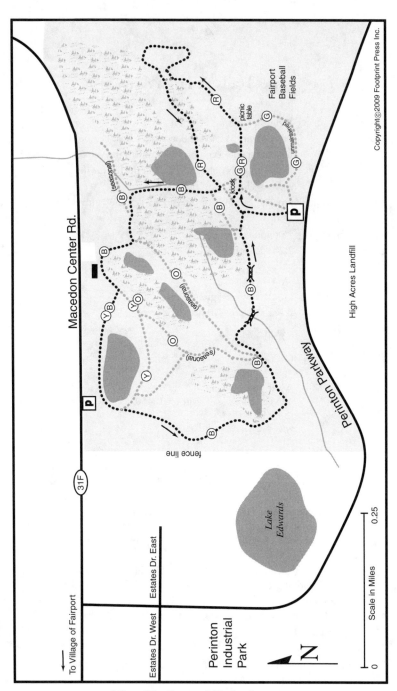

The Trails at High Acres

42

The Trails at High Acres

Location:	Perinton Parkway, Perinton
Directions:	From Route 31F (Macedon Center Road) east of Fairport, turn south onto Perinton Parkway. Pass the Waste Management facility to your right and watch to the left for the parking area for The Trails at High Acres.
Alternate Parking:	On 31F, east of Perinton Parkway, on the south side of the road.
Hiking Time:	75 minutes
Length:	2.2-mile loop
Difficulty:	
Surface:	Dirt and mowed grass paths
Trail Markings:	A few sign posts at intersections
Uses:	
Dogs:	OK on leash
Admission:	Free
Contact:	Waste Management of New York 425 Perinton Pkwy, Fairport 14450 (585) 223-6132 www.highacreslandfill.com

Part of the High Acres Landfill and Recycling Center of Waste Management, The Trails at High Acres wind through 150 acres of diverse ecosystems including a red maple hardwood swamp, a northern hardwood stand, a northern white cedar swamp, old farm fields and pastures, a flood plain forest, a rich mesophytic forest, and a deep emergent marsh. The 4 miles of trails were built in 1998 and offer the ability to view a wide variety of plants and animals. It's an especially good location for bird watching with diverse sightings such as sparrows, finches, and green herons.

It may seem strange to head to a landfill to hike, but this land sits across the street from the actual landfill and is a wonderful natural oasis. Some areas have fallen into disuse and are no longer maintained (such as the former green trail), and other areas (marked "seasonal" below) are wet or even under water after heavy rains.

Parking lot to Kiosk	0.1 mile
Red Trail Loop	0.7 mile
Kiosk to Orange Trail:	0.3 mile one way
Orange Trail Loop:	0.8 mile (seasonal)

Kiosk to Yellow Trail:	0.4 mile one way
Yellow Trail Loop:	0.5 mile (seasonal, un-bridged stream)
Blue Trail Loop:	1.8 miles
Blue Trail Extension:	0.2 mile one way (seasonal)

Trail Directions
- From the Perinton Parkway parking lot, head straight, passing a sign.
- Take a right at the "T."
- Bear right at the kiosk. (Some portions of the maps on the wooden signs are out of date.)
- Pass between two ponds.
- Bear left at the picnic table in a small clearing.
- Turn left onto the red trail. The path winds through a more heavily forested area.
- A trail leads off to your right, but continue straight.
- The path loops around to your left. At a "T," turn left.
- Come to a broad "Y." Bear right. You will begin to see glimpses of a pond on your right.
- At 0.75 mile, come to a "T." Turn right. (Left leads back to the kiosk area.)
- You are now on the blue trail. The trail bisects two ponds. (Although the paths in this section are fairly well maintained, they are very wet in spring, or after rain.)
- The trail bends to the left. (The blue trail extension veers off to the right.)
- At 1.0 mile, the trail splits into 3 different paths. Head right, towards a chain-link fence.
- Just before the fence, turn left.
- Cross a small footbridge over a creek.
- Turn left at a "T," then quickly come to a "Y" and bear right.
- You will now have a large pond, frequently used for fishing, on your left. Stay on the path closest to the pond as you pass a trail that leads to the alternate parking area.
- At 1.4 miles, you will pass another short path that leads to the alternate parking area. Stay on the main trail, and you will quickly come to a "Y." Bear right on the blue trail. (The yellow trail branches off to the left. It leads to the section of trail that is seasonally impassable.)
- The trail will eventually bear to the left, with a smaller path branching off to the right.
- Cross a small footbridge at 1.7 miles.
- Bear right when the path splits. (Left is part of the orange trail loop.)
- Cross a small bridge over a creek
- At 2.0 miles bear left at the "Y."
- Cross another bridge.
- Continue on main path. (You will pass two trails that lead to Perinton Parkway.)
- At a "T," turn right (S). This path will return to the parking area.

Date Hiked: _____
Notes:

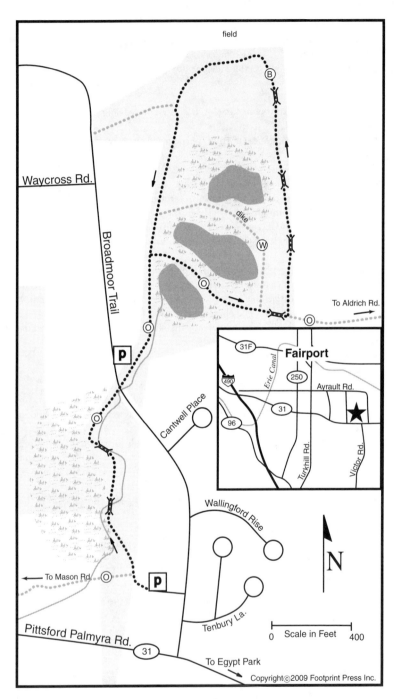

field

Waycross Rd.

Broadmoor Trail

To Aldrich Rd.

dike

31F

Fairport

Erie Canal

490

250

Ayrault Rd.

31

96

Turkhill Rd.

Victor Rd.

Cantwell Place

Wallingford Rise

N

To Mason Rd.

Tenbury La.

0   Scale in Feet   400

Pittsford Palmyra Rd.

31

To Egypt Park

Copyright©2009 Footprint Press Inc.

Wetlands Section

43

Wetlands Section - Crescent Trail

Location:	Broadmoor Trail, Perinton (off Route 31)
Directions:	From Route 490, head east on Route 31 (Palmyra Road). After Mason Road (shortly before leaving Monroe County) turn north on Broadmoor Trail. Take the first left onto a short dead-end road. Park at the end of the road.
Alternative Parking:	A grass off-street parking area, along Broadmoor Road where a small stream passes under the road.
Hiking Time:	50 minutes
Length:	1.6 mile loop
Difficulty:	
Surface:	Mowed-grass and dirt paths
Trail Markings:	3-inch Crescent Trail logo signs with trail color indicated in the bottom portion. The orange trail is blazed.
Uses:	
Dogs:	OK on leash
Admission:	Free
Contact:	The Crescent Trail Association, Inc.
	P.O. Box 1354, Fairport, NY 14450
	(585) 234-1621
	www.perinton.org/Departments/RandP/hikingctha/

This trail is a wonderful easy stroll through fields and woods. It passes near streams and ponds with active beaver, and you may notice trees the beaver have eaten. Beaver dens may be visible, and many beaver trails are in evidence. The ponds are also home to ducks, Canada geese, and great blue herons. With the combination of ponds, grasslands, and woods, this area is home to many birds, making it a birder's paradise.

Trail Directions
- From the dead-end road, bear right (N), heading into the tree line to find the trail. (There are no signs or blazes marking the trail.)
- Continue straight on the orange trail. (The orange trail also turns left here.)
- The stream will appear to your left.
- Cross the stream on a small wooden bridge.
- Cross the stream on the second bridge.
- Cross Broadmoor Trail. Continue straight (NE) on the orange trail.
- Pass the first pond on the right. (Houses will be on your left.)

- At 0.5 mile, reach a junction. Turn right (SE) and follow the orange trail, passing between two ponds.
- Pass an unmarked trail to your left. (It's the white trail.) Continue straight and cross a bridge.
- Soon, turn left on an unblazed trail. (It's the blue trail. The orange trail continues straight, leading to Aldrich Road.)
- Cross a wooden bridge.
- Cross a second, then a third wooden bridge.
- Pass a farm field on the right.
- Bear left. (To the right is a side trail leading to Broadmoor Trail.)
- Pass a house on the right and a pond on the left.
- Continue straight on the orange trail. (The orange trail also heads left here.)
- Cross Broadmoor Trail.
- Cross two small wooden bridges.
- Bear left when the orange trail bends right, to return to the dead-end street parking area.

Date Hiked: _____
Notes:

Northeast
Section

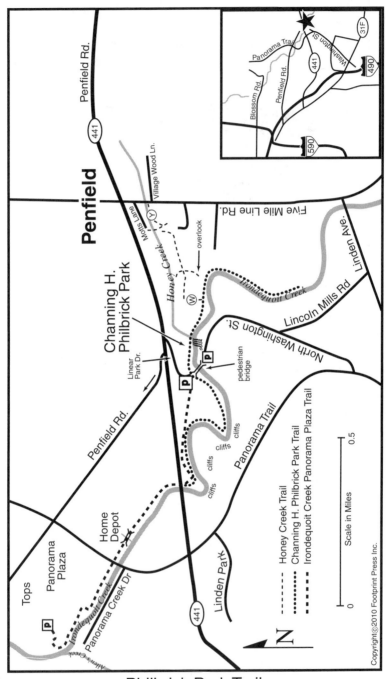

Philbrick Park Trails

44

Philbrick Park Trails

Location:	Channing H. Philbrick Park (formerly Linear Park), Penfield
Directions:	From Route 441 (Penfield Road) turn south on Linear Park Drive. The parking area for Channing H. Philbrick Park is at the end of Linear Park Drive.
Alternate Parking:	At the end of North Washington Street In the Tops parking lot at Panorama Plaza In the Home Depot parking lot on Panorama Trail
Hiking Time:	45 minutes round trip - Channing H. Philbrick Park Trail 40 minutes round trip - Irondequoit Creek Panorama Plaza Trail 30 minute round trip, side trip - Honey Creek Trail
Length:	1.5-miles round trip - Channing H. Philbrick Park Trail 2.0-miles round trip - Irondequoit Creek Panorama Plaza Trail 1.0-mile round trip - Honey Creek Trail
Difficulty:	🥾🥾🥾🥾
Surface:	Dirt paths, wooden bridges and steps on the Channing H. Philbrick Park Trail and the Honey Creek Trail Crushed gravel on Irondequoit Creek Panorama Plaza Trail
Trail Markings:	None
Uses:	🚶🚴♿ (biking and handicapped access on Irondequoit Creek Panorama Plaza Trail only)
Dogs:	OK on leash
Admission:	Free
Contact:	Town of Penfield Parks & Recreation 3100 Atlantic Ave., Penfield, NY 14526 (585) 340-8600 www.penfield.org/index.php?pr=Town_Trails

This area of Irondequoit Creek is known as "The Falls" or "The Hollow" because the creek drops 90 feet in one mile, creating a series of cascading waterfalls. (Many other local waterfalls are detailed in *200 Waterfalls in Central & Western New York - A Finders' Guide*.) The indians called this area SGOH-SA-IS-THAH.

Daniel Penfield settled the area and built the first mill in 1800. It was soon followed by many mills. If you look closely along the creek banks, you'll see some foundations that still remain. The years 1800-1840 were a time of rapid settlement and growth, encouraged by Mr. Penfield's policy of accepting wheat and other farm products for his mills in lieu of mortgage payments until a farmer had enough time to become established.

The businesses built along this section of Irondequoit Creek included flour mills, sawmills, an ashery, an oil mill and soap factory, distilleries, wool and clothing mills, grist mills, a tannery, a blacksmithy, and a slaughter house. Produce from the mills was shipped via Tryon (see Ellison Park on page 198 for more information on Tryon.) to Charlotte, then transported across Lake Ontario to Canada. When the Erie Canal was built it was hauled to the ports at Fairport and Pittsford for shipment to markets in the east.

One of many cascades along this stretch of Irondequoit Creek.

Formerly called Linear Park, this park was renamed Channing H. Philbrick Park in honor of the man who was Penfield's Town Supervisor for many years.

Three trails are described. In 2005 the crushed gravel Irondequoit Creek Panorama Plaza Trail was opened for hiking, biking, and handicapped access between Philbrick Park and Panorama Plaza. Expect to hear some road noise along this easy trail. West of the pedestrian bridge which spans Irondequoit Creek between Philbrick Park and North Washington Street is a portion of the Channing H. Philbrick Park Trail along Irondequoit Creek with views of towering sand cliffs. This dirt trail continues to the east, paralleling the creek and offers a pleasant, quiet walk. A branch off this forms the Honey Creek Trail which leads into the village of Penfield. Combine these trails for a walk past the cascading waterfalls through the Irondequoit Creek valley.

Trail Directions (Channing H. Philbrick Park Trail)
• At the eastern edge of the parking area, look for the trail kiosk. Walk upstream on the wide dirt path, keeping Irondequoit Creek to your right.
• Cross a small tributary.
• Pass a small trail on the left that leads to private property.

- Pass the white-blazed Honey Creek Trail to the left. (See the directions below if you wish to take this as a side trip.)
- Cross 2 bridges, then climb 6 steps.
- Cross 2 bridges, then 2 boardwalks.
- Cross a wooden bridge labeled Shelley Bridge, then cross another boardwalk.
- The trail ends at a steep climb.
- Turn around and return to the parking area.

Side Trip Directions (Honey Creek Trail)
- From the Channing H. Philbrick Park Trail, turn left and follow the white blazes uphill on the Honey Creek Trail.
- Pass a bench on the left.
- Pass a side trail to the right that goes to a viewpoint above the creek.
- Pass a side trail to the left that goes to a private house.
- Turn right at the "T." (Left leads to parking behind Nothnagle at the end of Motts Lane.)

Sand cliffs carved by Irondequoit Creek.

- Turn left to follow the yellow-blazed trail to Five Mile Line Road. (Straight leads to apartments.)
- Turn around and retrace your steps back to the Channing H. Philbrick Park Trail.

Trail Directions (Irondequoit Creek Panorama Plaza Trail)
- From the Philbrick Park parking area, head west toward the playground equipment.
- Follow the gravel footpath. (A dirt path will be parallel to the gravel trail, but closer to the creek.)
- Pass a metal fence and cross a footbridge. Stay on the gravel path.
- Cross a second footbridge.
- The gravel path and dirt path merge.
- Cross under the Route 441 bridge.
- Cross a wooden bridge next to Home Depot.
- Cross under the Panorama Trail road bridge.
- Reach the end of the trail with a small loop and a good parking lot.
- Turn around and retrace your steps to Channing Philbrick Park.

Date Hiked: _____
Notes:

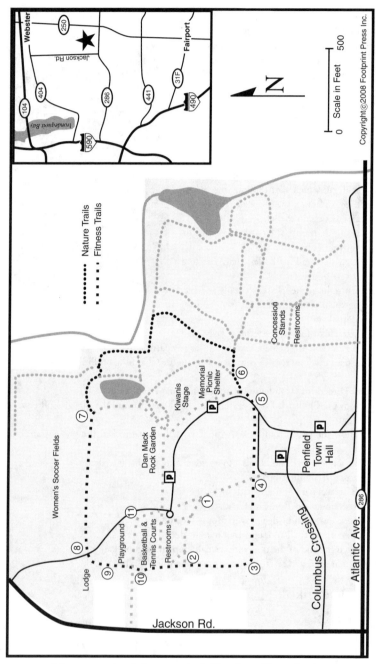

Veteran's Memorial Park - Penfield

180

45

Veteran's Memorial Park - Penfield

Location:	Veteran's Memorial Park, 3100 Atlantic Ave., Penfield
Directions:	Head east on Browncroft Boulevard (Route 286) until it turns into Atlantic Avenue. Turn north into Veteran's Memorial Park between Jackson Road and Fairport Nine Mile Point Road (Route 250). Pass the town hall building and park just beyond the picnic shelter.
Alternative Parking:	The parking area behind the town hall
Hiking Time:	30 minutes
Length:	0.8 mile loop
Difficulty:	
Surface:	Mowed-grass, dirt, boardwalk and paved paths
Trail Markings:	None
Uses:	🏃 🎿 ♿
Dogs:	OK on leash
Admission:	Free
Contact:	Town of Penfield Parks & Recreation 3100 Atlantic Ave., Penfield, NY 14526 (585) 340-8600 www.penfield.org/index.php?pr=Town_Trails

Developed from land purchased in 1980 and 1990, Penfield's Veteran's Memorial Park opened in 1995. Making optimum use of its land, the park is home to baseball diamonds, football/soccer fields, picnic facilities, tennis and basketball courts, a playground, a fishing pond, a rock garden, physical fitness exercise stations, and a hiking trail.

The trail described here begins in a wood lot (arboretum), then follows a paved path around the perimeter of the park. Along the paved portion you will pass several exercise stations. Numbered posts along the way draw your attention to labeled trees and bushes.

The park contains several paved path loops (part of which are used for this hiking trail) which provide a suitable surface for strollers, wheelchairs, and in-line skates.

Trail Directions
• From the parking area, head towards the flagpole (E). Go up the steps and past the veteran's memorial.
• Look for the trailhead post at the edge of the woods, behind the picnic shelter.

- Pass post 34 (wild honeysuckle) on the right. (Going left takes you on a path back to the picnic area.)
- At the junction, turn right (E) into the woods.
- Pass a trail to the right and head downhill.
- The trail will fork. Bear left, passing #35 (mayapple) and #28 (white ash).
- Cross a small wooden bridge.
- At the "T," turn left. The creek will be on your right.
- Stay on the main trail, as several smaller trails branch off.
- Traverse a short boardwalk.
- Pass post #24 (poison ivy).
- Reach a "T" at 0.3 mile. Turn left (NW). (Right dead-ends.)
- Pass post 13 (Douglas fir).
- Reach the paved path and turn right (NW).
- The paved path will quickly split. Follow the path that goes straight ahead, running between two athletic fields.
- Continue along the path. Past the crosswalk, you will turn left on the paved path. The lodge will be on your right.
- Pass the playground and tennis courts on your left.
- Continue past 2 branches of a paved path to the left.
- Just after 0.5 mile, the paved path ends. Turn left (E) and follow the tree line between baseball fields.
- Cross a paved path.
- At the park road, turn left (E) to return to the parking area.

Date Hiked: _____

Notes:

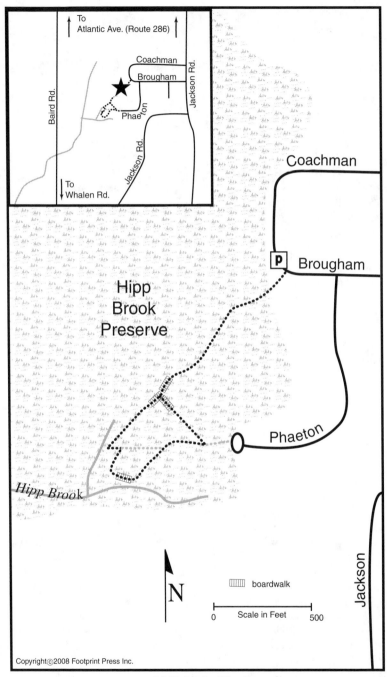

Wild Iris Trail

46

Wild Iris Trail

Location:	Hipp Brook Preserve, Penfield
Directions:	From Route 286 (Atlantic Ave.), west of Route 250, turn south on Jackson Road. Take the 4th right onto Brougham Drive and park where the road begins to bend right near the sign for "Wild Iris Trail."
Alternative Parking:	Continue past the trailhead and park along Coachman Dr.
Hiking Time:	20 minutes
Length:	0.5 mile loop
Difficulty:	
Surface:	Woodchip path and boardwalks
Trail Markings:	None
Uses:	
Dogs:	OK on leash (pick up after your dog)
Admission:	Free
Contact:	Town of Penfield Parks & Recreation
	3100 Atlantic Ave., Penfield, NY 14526
	(585) 340-8600
	www.penfield.org/index.php?pr=Town_Trails
	Genesee Land Trust
	500 East Avenue, Suite 200, Rochester, NY 14607
	(585) 256-2130
	www.geneseelandtrust.org

Hipp Brook Preserve covers 94 acres of wooded swamp, cattail marsh, flowing stream (Hipp Brook), and upland grasslands owned by the Genesee Land Trust. It's home to great horned owls, wood ducks, numerous species of butterflies, frogs and salamanders. While wild irises are rare along the trail, they bloom in other parts of the preserve. Other wildflowers abound, including cardinal flower, marsh marigold, and closed gentian. The entire property is very wet in the spring.

Trail Directions
• From Brougham Drive, head to the trailhead at the edge of the woods.
• Proceed along wood chip path.
• Pass a bench at 0.1 mile.
• You will soon arrive at a boardwalk.
• When the boardwalk splits, bear right. (Left serves as the return path.)
• Pass a small path on your left.

- The trail will bear left and you will soon come to a 2nd boardwalk.
- At the "T," turn right.
- Shortly after the turn, the trail will split again. Bear left. (Right leads to Phaeton Drive.)
- Reach the boardwalk.
- When boardwalk splits, bear right.
- Continue on the wood chip trail until you arrive at the trailhead.

Date Hiked: _____

Notes:

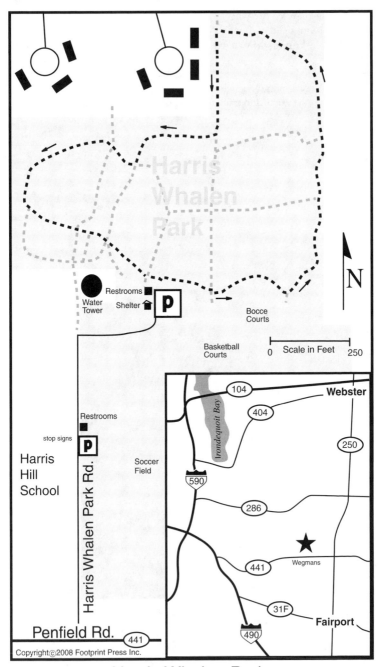

Harris Whalen Park

47

Harris Whalen Trail

Location:	Harris Whalen Park, Penfield
Directions:	Head east from Interstate 490 on Penfield Road (Route 441). Turn north onto Harris Whalen Drive shortly before the Route 250 intersection. Drive up the hill to the parking area to the right of the water tower.

Alternative Parking: None
Hiking Time: 30 minutes
Length: 0.9 mile loop
Difficulty: 🥾 🥾 🥾 🥾 🥾 🥾

Surface: Dirt and mulched paths
Trail Markings: None
Uses:

Dogs: OK on leash
Admission: Free
Contact: Town of Penfield Parks & Recreation
3100 Atlantic Ave., Penfield, NY 14526
(585) 340-8600
www.penfield.org/index.php?pr=Town_Trails

This trail winds through a stand of mixed forest at the top of Harris Hill. The trails range from 2 to 10-feet wide and are easy to follow even though they're not marked or blazed.

Trail Directions
• Walk into the woods from the northeast corner of the parking lot.
• Quickly, turn right (E).
• Pass a trail to the right. (It leads to bocce courts.)
• Stay inside the woods and head downhill (E).
• The trail will bend left (N).
• Pass two trails to the left.
• The trail bends left and houses come into view.
• At the "T," turn left. (Right leaves park property and heads to houses.)
• Head uphill.
• Turn right at the next intersection (before a bench).
• Turn right at the next intersection and head down a steep hill.
• At the bottom, pass a trail on the left, then bear left (straight heads to houses).
• Turn right onto the next trail.

- At the "Y," bear left.
- Pass an intersection and climb the hill.
- Continue straight through a junction of 3 trails. (The water tower is to your right.)
- Bear right toward the restrooms and return to the parking lot.

Date Hiked: _____

Notes:

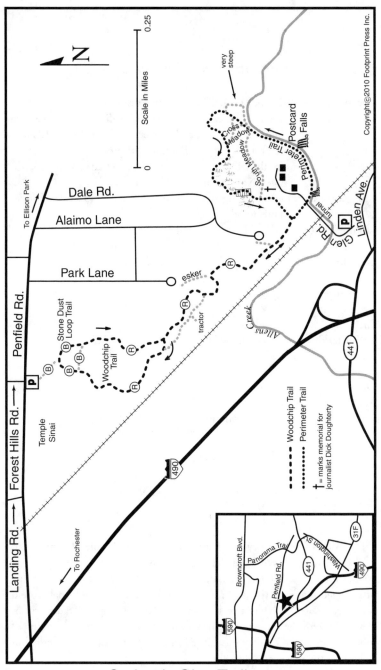

Corbett's Glen Trails

189

48

Corbett's Glen Trails

Location:	Corbett's Glen Nature Park, Brighton
Directions:	From I-490 exit to Route 441 heading east. At the first light, turn left on Linden Avenue, then turn immediately left on Glen Road. Look for the green and gold signs on the left and right "Park Here to Curve for Corbett's Glen Nature Park."

Alternative Parking: A parking area on Penfield Road, across from Forest Hills Road.

Hiking Time:	1 hour loop on Woodchip Trail
	30 minutes loop on Perimeter Trail
Length:	1.4 mile loop on Woodchip Trail
	0.7 mile loop on Perimeter Trail
Difficulty:	👟 👟 👟 👟
Surface:	Paved road, gravel and dirt trails
Trail Markings:	Green and gold signs and blue and white signs
Uses:	🚶
Dogs:	OK on leash
Admission:	Free
Contact:	Town of Brighton, Parks & Recreation
	220 Idlewood Road, Rochester, NY 14618
	(585) 784-5260
	www.townofbrighton.org/index.asp?nid=220
	Allens Creek/Corbett's Glen Preservation Group
	PO Box 25717, Rochester, NY 14625-0717
	(585) 385-2293
	www.corbettsglen.org

The Allens Creek valley is a natural oasis in the middle of a suburban landscape. It was saved from development by the efforts of many caring people and officially became a nature park in 1999. Native Americans had one of their major footpaths through this valley and a sacred burial ground was documented to be located here in the 1800s. European traders established ties with the Indians at nearby Indian Landing. With the coming of more Europeans, the valley was turned into farmland and mills were built to harness the power of Allens Creek.

An old tractor can be found along the Woodchip Trail.

The first wooden railroad trestle was built over Allens Creek in 1851 for the Rochester and Syracuse Railway. Pre Civil War, a powder mill, owned by John Tyron, operated in the glen to produce blasting powder. In 1889 Patrick Corbett bought the land that today is called Corbett's Glen. He built a large farm and irrigated his crops with water from Allens Creek using a unique system. For decades he operated the glen as a privately run picnic ground. He built dancing pavilions, picnic tables, baseball diamonds, and beer halls (in the midst of prohibition!). Paying 25 cents per person, obscure social clubs and businesses such as Eastman Kodak Company used the glen for weekend parties.

In 1956, part of the glen was purchased by Howard Meath who operated Camp Hideaway for children. He staged small concerts in the 1970s. Between the 1930s and 1970s the area was a target of vandalism and Allens Creek became polluted from a nearby waste disposal plant, creating an environmental disaster. It wasn't until the 1980s that a Pure Waters Project helped clean up the land and water.

In the 1990s we came very close to losing Corbett's Glen to make way for industrial parks and expensive housing. The Meath and Corbett families were looking to sell their land and developers salivated. But residents of the area banded together to form the Allens Creek / Corbett's Glen Preservation Group and eventually the Town of Brighton and Genesee Land Trust joined forces in the first ever public-private collaboration in the Greater Rochester area to acquire a 17.7 acre parcel of land in Corbett's Glen.

In 2001 Brighton more than doubled the park's land when it purchased a 34-acre parcel just north of the glen and south of Penfield Road. In 2008 adjacent land was threatened with development of a two-story industrial building and parking lot. Again, the Allens Creek / Corbett's Glen Preservation Group persevered. Their preservation work is far from done, so if you'd like to contribute funds or volunteer time, contact either the Genesee Land Trust or the Allens Creek / Corbett's Glen Preservation Group.

Geologically, Corbett's Glen owes its existence to the glaciers that once covered this area. As the glacier melted it formed a large lake called Iroquois Lake. It was bigger than Lake Ontario is today. Streams drained into this lake and widened their valleys. As the land sprung back, released from the weight of the ice, the streams cut deeper causing a series of terraces. 20 or more of these terraces have been mapped in Corbett's Glen.

On your way into Corbett's Glen you'll walk through a railroad tunnel with Allens Creek bubbling beside you. This tunnel was built in 1882 to replace the original trestle. Limestone was quarried from bedrock at the edge of the glen. At the end of the tunnel is the first waterfall, a cascade over jagged dolomite outcroppings. A short walk on the easy Perimeter Trail takes you to the second waterfall (Postcard Falls). (To explore other area waterfalls, pick up a copy of *200 Waterfalls in Central & Western New York - A Finders' Guide*.) Keep an eye out for wildlife. Foxes, owls, birds, mink, opossum, turkey, and deer are all prevalent. Beyond the waterfall, continue on the Perimeter Trail through a meadow surrounded by steep slopes.

For a longer hike, follow the red-blazed Woodchip Trail for a loop toward Penfield Road. You'll find dolomite stone set along the trails as sitting stools.

Perimeter Trail Directions
- Walk downhill on Glen Road and continue through the tunnel.
- You'll find the first waterfall at the far end of the tunnel. It's a jagged edged, 6-foot cascade.
- Bear right, following the creek on the 8-foot-wide gravel path.
- Pass a picnic table.
- Reach a wide grassy area. Follow your ears to the right to find an 5-foot high jagged, multi-level cascade filling the full width of Allens Creek (Postcard Falls).
- The path becomes mulched.
- Pass the South Meadow Trail to the left. (Note: along the South Meadow Trail you'll find a bench and stone memorial to Dick Dougherty.)

- Pass a steep trail on your right.
- To the left, pass the Cross Meadow Trail. (Take this trail if you wish to avoid the steep section of the Perimeter Trail. This is especially recommended if the trails are wet.)
- Continue straight, heading steeply uphill. Climb to the top. Pass a side trail on the right.
- Head down the steep trail. Bear left half-way down. (The trail to the right passes a broken fence and leads to private property.)
- Pass Cross Meadow Trail on your left.
- Pass a small side trail that leads into a ravine and to private homes.
- The trail returns to crushed stone.
- Cross a boardwalk.
- Pass the South Meadow Trail to the left.
- Turn left at the "T" to return to Glen Road. (Or, turn right to follow the Woodchip Trail.)

Woodchip Trail Directions
- Walk downhill on Glen Road and continue through the tunnel.
- You'll find the first waterfall at the far end of the tunnel. It's a jagged edged, 3-foot cascade.
- Turn left, following the red arrow.
- Pass a trail on the right (Perimeter Trail) and head uphill.
- Pass a long, 8-foot-high fence on the right.
- Traverse in and out of a gully, then climb some stone steps.
- Pass a small side trail to the right.
- Come to a "T" and turn left following the red blazes. (The side trail to the right goes along an esker.)
- Pass an unmarked side trail on the left. (Note: a quick trip on this trail leads to an old tractor.)
- Bear left at the "Y" junction.
- Pass the Stone Dust Loop Trail to the right (blue blazed).
- Pass a trail on the left, (it leads to the Penfield Road parking area) and begin your return loop.
- Pass the Stone Dust Loop Trail on the right (blue blazed).
- Pass a trail to the right. (It's the red-blazed trail you took on the outward leg.).
- Pass the unmarked tractor trail to the right, then two side trails to the left.
- Continue straight, passing the Perimeter Trail on the left.
- Return through the tunnel to Glen Road.

Date Hiked: _____

Notes:

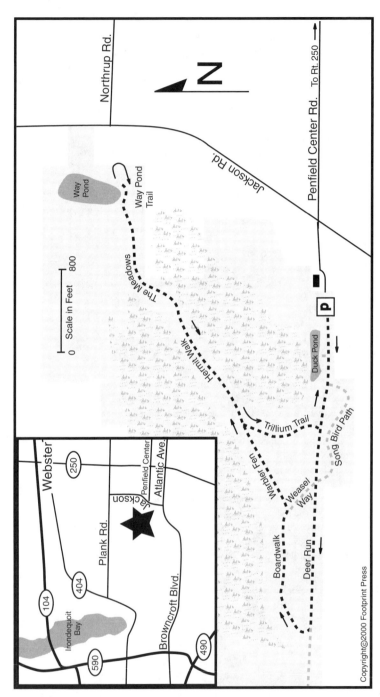

194 Thousand Acre Swamp Trail

49

Thousand Acre Swamp Trail

Location:	Jackson Road, Penfield
Directions:	From Jackson Road (between Atlantic Avenue and Plank Road), turn west into Thousand Acre Swamp. Drive into the sanctuary parking area.
Alternative Parking:	None
Hiking Time:	1.5 hours
Length:	2.6 mile loop
Difficulty:	🥾
Surface:	Dirt path and boardwalks
Trail Markings:	Wooden signs
Uses:	🚶
Dogs:	Pets are NOT allowed
Admission:	Free
Contact:	The Nature Conservancy 315 Alexander Street, Rochester, NY 14604 (585) 546-8030 www.nature.org/wherewework/northamerica/states/ newyork/preserves/art13583.html

White trilliums, ferns, and blue violets are among the 500 plant species known to inhabit the Thousand Acre Swamp Sanctuary, along with large hardwood species of northern red oak, white oak, sugar maple, and black cherry. They share the land with deer, rabbit, red and grey fox, muskrat, opossum, mink, eastern coyote, and over one-hundred forty-seven species of birds. It's no wonder that the Central and Western New York Chapter of the Nature Conservancy chose these lands for preservation.

The Thousand Acre Swamp Sanctuary is a great place to watch marsh life. It's easy to spot animal footprints in the mud and get an up-close look at frogs, snapping turtles, and nesting geese. Bring binoculars for the best viewing. Local legend has it that the sanctuary was once the home of a hermit who wanted to get away from the world.

Trails can be muddy and in wet weather, insect repellent is advised. Guided hikes, offered on weekends from April through the end of October, cover a variety of interesting subjects such as wildflowers, coyotes, hidden worlds, and photography. Contact the Nature Conservancy for the latest schedule, or pick one up at the trail head kiosk.

The Nature Conservancy is a non-profit international membership organization committed to global preservation of natural diversity. The Central and Western New York Chapter has protected more than 13,000 acres and owns and manages 29 nature sanctuaries in this region.

The trail described here is an easy walk through forests and swamps. Your feet will stay dry thanks to the many boardwalks.

Canada geese nest at Way Pond in Thousand Acre Swamp each spring.

Trail Directions
- From the parking area, head west across the boardwalk on the Entrance Trail.
- Pass the information kiosk.
- Pass a small trail on the right to Duck Pond.
- Cross another boardwalk.
- Stay on Deer Run and pass the junctions of Song Bird Trail, Trillium Trail, and Weasel Way.
- At 0.4 mile, turn right on Boardwalk Trail to cross the swamp.

- Continue straight onto Warbler Fen.
- At 0.7 mile, bear left on Hermit Walk to wander through the woods.
- At 1.2 miles, turn right (E) on the Meadow Trail and walk the edge of a mowed meadow filled with bluebird houses.
- Turn right (E) onto Way Pond Trail.
- Cross another meadow then enter woods.
- The trail skirts the south end of Way Pond and then dead-ends at 1.5 miles. (In spring look for turtles and nesting geese on the island.)
- Turn around and walk back along The Way Pond Trail, The Meadow Trail, and Hermit Walk.
- Turn left onto Trillium Trail at 2.2 miles.
- Reach a "T" and turn left onto Deer Run and follow the Entrance Trail back to the parking area.

Date Hiked: _____

Notes:

Ellison Park

Irondequoit Creek winds through this wooded, hilly, 447-acre park. (For a wonderful paddling adventure down Irondequoit Creek, pick up a copy of *Take A Paddle - Western New York Quiet Water for Canoes & Kayaks*.) The first trail takes you to a little used, remote area of the park. The second trail takes you around the historic section of Ellison Park highlighting some of the remnants of the lost city of Tryon.

The lost city of Tryon was the dream of one man, Salmon Tryon. In 1797 he found what he thought was the ideal location for his city. It had everything needed to prosper: waterpower, timberland, a strategic location on land and water routes, a good harbor, and an increasing population.

However, Salmon needed cash within a year and sold it to his brother, John and his partners. They built a business complex consisting of a warehouse, a five-story mercantile, a distillery, a factory for making ash, and a shipping dock with boats. The distillery and ashery were first to be put into operation. Clearing trees, then burning them produced potash which was in great demand as an early fertilizer. Sacks of grain were cooked down into liquor in the distillery.

Within the park is Fort Schuyler. The existing fort was erected as a WPA (Work Projects Administration) project in 1938 to commemorate the original colonial trading post that stood in this vicinity in 1721 — 75 years before Tryon was founded. However, the original Fort Schuyler was abandoned after only one year because it became too difficult to keep it supplied from Albany.

Where did Tryon go? Its decline began with John Tryon's death in 1807. In the midst of trying to settle the estate, his executor also died. The stone warehouse and dock were in dire need of repairs. Money was scarce and the property as a whole was impossible to sell. So the distillery was dismantled and individual lots were sold.

In addition to these problems, the War of 1812 added to the decline of commerce on Lake Ontario. Construction of the Erie Canal was the final blow to Tryon. The canal bypassed Irondequoit Bay and provided a safer route without the need to worry about the storms and high winds on the lake.

Ownership changed several times over the years until the twentieth century when residential areas in the town of Brighton sprang up in place of the old farmsteads. Monroe County bought most of what had been Tryon from the Ellison family in 1927 for the creation of Ellison Park.

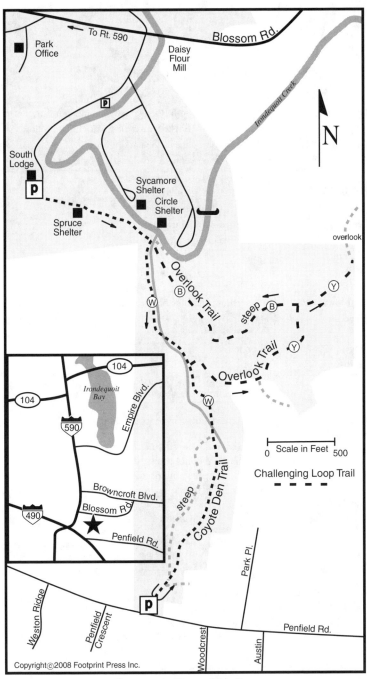

Coyote Den Trail

50

Coyote Den Trail

Location:	Ellison Park, Penfield
Directions:	Turn south off Blossom Road where the blue sign lists South Lodge and Spruce Shelter. Take the first right and follow the road past South Lodge to the parking area.
Alternative Parking:	Parking lot along Penfield Road marked by a "Monroe County Ellison Park Trailhead" sign.
Hiking Time:	50 minutes (easy round trip)
	60 minutes (challenging loop)
Length:	1.7 miles (easy round trip)
	2.1 miles (challenging loop)
Difficulty:	🥾🥾 easy trail 🥾🥾🥾🥾 challenging loop
Surface:	dirt path
Trail Markings:	White, yellow, and blue blazes. Blue signs on wooden posts.
Uses:	🚶
Dogs:	OK on leash
Admission:	Free, open 6 AM - 11 PM
Contact:	Monroe County Parks Department
	171 Reservoir Avenue, Rochester, NY 14620
	(585) 256-4950
	www.monroecounty.gov/parks-ellison.php

Coyote Den Trail leads into an undeveloped, forested area in the southern section of Ellison Park. You'll walk a gradual uphill through the bottom of a ravine beside a small stream, with sharp hills rising all around. Return via the same route for an easy hike or take a yellow-blazed side trail to the top of the surrounding hills for a challenging loop with a panoramic view of a quarry pond. Many large trees can be found in this area, including a white oak listed in the National Registry of Big Trees.

Eastern coyote, red fox, and deer inhabit this park. If you see canine tracks it's more fun to assume they're from coyote than from the common dog.

Trail Directions
- From the parking area, walk southeast to the left of Spruce Shelter, with Irondequoit Creek to your left.
- The path will become well-worn. Pass a wooden post with a small blue "Coyote Den Trail" sign.
- Keep Irondequoit Creek to your left and a hill to your right.

• The next sign post directs you across a small wooden bridge and uphill to the Overlook Trail or right (to the right of the tributary creek) for the Coyote Den Trail. Continue right on Coyote Den Trail.

• Cross the creek three times on small wooden bridges.

• Turn right onto the 4th bridge to keep following Coyote Den Trail. (Straight is the Overlook Trail, part of the return trip.)

• Stay in the base of the ravine, going straight on the white-blazed trail. (A side trail to the right leads steeply up an esker and returns to the main trail.)

• At 0.8 mile, reach the trailhead parking lot on Penfield Road. Don't miss looking at the large white oak to your right.

• Turn around and follow the white-blazed trail, retracing your steps. (A small trail to the right goes nowhere. Twice you'll pass the junction with the esker trail on the left.)

EASY route

• When you reach the junction with the yellow trail (shortly after the first wooden bridge), turn left to continue on Coyote Den Trail. Follow the white blazes back to the parking lot.

STEEP route

• Immediately after the first wooden bridge, turn right (S) for the more strenuous Overlook Trail return loop. It will begin level, in a gully, in a deep forest.

• Pass a short side trail to the right.

• Start a gradual uphill.

• At 1.5 miles you'll reach a "T." Turn right on the yellow-blazed trail. You'll come to a lookout over a working Dolomite quarry that's now filled with water. (The trail continues down to water level but it's a narrow trail and is on private land.)

• Turn around and retrace your steps to the last junction.

• Go straight on the blue-blazed Overlook Trail. (Left is the yellow-blazed trail you already walked. In winter or in the rain, take this yellow trail back down.)

• Follow the top of the ridge then head downhill, gradually at first, then very steeply.

• Reach water level, cross a small bridge, and continue straight (NW) along the banks of Irondequoit Creek to the parking area.

Date Hiked: _____

Notes:

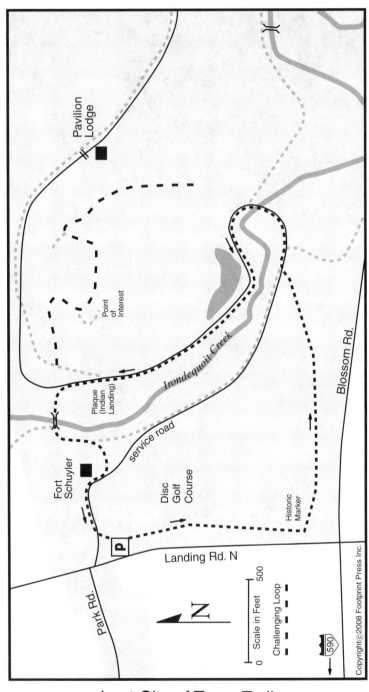

Pavilion
Lodge

Point
of
Interest

Irondequoit Creek

Plaque
(Indian
Landing)

service road

Fort
Schuyler

Disc
Golf
Course

Historic
Marker

Blossom Rd.

P

Landing Rd. N

Park Rd.

N

Scale in Feet
0   500

Challenging Loop

590

Copyright©2008 Footprint Press Inc.

Lost City of Tryon Trail

51

Lost City of Tryon Trail

Location:	Ellison Park, Penfield
Directions:	From Blossom Road, turn north on North Landing Road.
	A parking area will be on the right (E) side of the road
Alternative Parking:	None
Hiking Time:	40 minutes (easy loop)
	50 minutes (challenging loop)
Length:	1.4 miles (easy loop)
	1.6 miles (challenging loop)
Difficulty:	🥾🥾 easy loop 🥾🥾🥾🥾 challenging loop
Surface:	Mowed-grass and paved path
Trail Markings:	None
Uses:	🚶 🎿 (ski easy loop only)
Dogs:	OK on leash
Admission:	Free
Contact:	Monroe County Parks Department
	171 Reservoir Avenue, Rochester, NY 14620
	(585) 256-4950
	www.monroecounty.gov/parks-ellison.php

The 1.4-mile easy loop hugs Irondequoit Creek, while the more challenging 1.6-mile loop takes a detour to climb a very steep sand cliff to a forested ridge. Both loops take you past Fort Schulyer and a couple of historic markers.

Trail Directions

- From the parking area, head right (S) uphill across a grass field toward the corner of North Landing and Blossom Roads.
- Pass an old spring and cattail area on your right. Across the road is the newly remodeled "Old Tryon House," originally built in the late 1700's. Be on the lookout for flying frisbees! You are traversing a section of the park that is almost as popular with "disk golfers" in the summer as it is with sledders in the winter.
- Pass an historic plaque near the corner of Blossom and North Landing Roads that is surrounded by an array of colorful flowers and plants.
- Continue toward Blossom Road, then bear left before the road, heading downhill, toward Irondequoit Creek.
- At the bottom of the hill, continue straight, passing through pine trees, until you reach a small paved service road.
- Take a right at the road and follow it as it crosses Irondequoit Creek. This section of the park is a favorite of both dogs and their human friends.

- The path veers left, so the creek is now on your left.

EASY Route
- Continue to follow the path as it runs parallel to Irondequoit Creek.
  ATTENTION: This section of the trail is routinely under several inches of water after heavy rainfall, so plan accordingly!
- Nearing a second bridge spanning the creek, you will see a historical marker embedded in a large rock, across the field to your left. Cross the field and read the plaque.
  HISTORY: You are now standing on the site of Indian Landing. Water was by far the easiest way for the Indians to travel. Indians coming north from the Mississippi and Susquehanna Rivers would travel down the Genesee River to the rapids at Red Creek in Genesee Valley Park. (These rapids disappeared when the Court St. Dam was built to raise the water level for the Erie Canal.) To avoid the rapids and the three falls of the Genesee River, the Indians would portage along the route of Highland Ave. to this spot on Irondequoit Creek. From here they could go out through Irondequoit Bay to Lake Ontario. This was a very important trade route for the Indians.

STEEP, Challenging Route
- As the paved path bends left, follow the dirt path that branches off and heads steeply uphill - climb carefully and watch your footing!
- Once you've reached the top of the hill, walk along the ridgeline, bearing left at each junction. Keep the swampy pond far below to your left.
- Follow the trail as it makes a steep descent from the ridge. Stay on the main trail as you reach the base of the hill. (Another trail branches off to the left after a wooden bench.)
- As you emerge from the forest, bear right and head across the field towards the plaque.

BOTH Trails Meet Here.
- Cross the bridge over Irondequoit Creek and bear left. (Right goes to a horse farm.)
- At the "Y," bear right and head uphill.
- Pass a replica of Fort Schulyer on your right
- Once past the fort, bear left, and go uphill to the parking lot.

Date Hiked: _____

Notes:

204

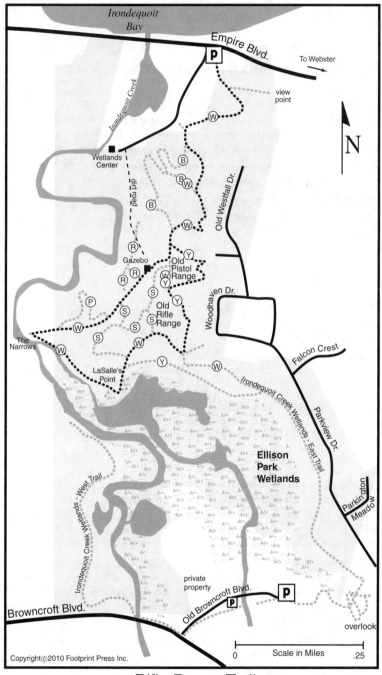

Rifle Range Trail

52

Rifle Range Trail

Location:	1129 Empire Boulevard (Route 404), Penfield
Directions:	Head east from Interstate 590 on Empire Boulevard into the dugway at the south end of Irondequoit Bay. Park in the gravel parking lot east of MacGregor's Grill & Taproom at 1129 Empire Boulevard.
Alternative Parking:	Old Browncroft Blvd. (for a longer hike)
Hiking Time:	2 hour loop
Length:	3.4 mile loop on Rifle Range Trail
Difficulty:	🥾🥾🥾🥾
Surface:	Dirt trail
Trail Markings:	Colored blazes
Uses:	🚶
Dogs:	OK
Admission:	Free
Contact:	Monroe County Parks Department 171 Reservoir Avenue, Rochester, NY 14620 (585) 256-4950
	Genesee Valley Chapter of the Adirondack Mountain Club www.gvc-adk.org
	Penfield Trails Committee www.penfield.org/index.php?pr=Trails

This is a heavily wooded and a steep terrain area making it a gem to hike. Not only for the beautiful woodland setting, but for its unusual history. Beginning in 1933, this area was home to an elegant, gated gun club consisting of a large 2-story Georgian style clubhouse with a gazebo. The ranges were used by club members and also by the N.Y. State Police, Rochester Police Dept. and the N.Y. National Guard. The area was last used for military training during the Korean War.

Within the steep hills were several ranges for rifle, pistol, shot gun and machine gun practice. If you look carefully you can still find some of the target mechanisms and safety trenches. Several sets of cement steps once led shooters to the front of the range. Unfortunately, the clubhouse is long gone, but a rebuilt gazebo remains, sitting atop a small hill that offered a good overall view of the ranges.

The trail was first conceived by Steve Webber and Joe Schuler in the early 1980s. In 1994 the property was purchased by Monroe County and became the responsibility of Ellison Park. Beginning in 1995, the initial trail was adopted by the

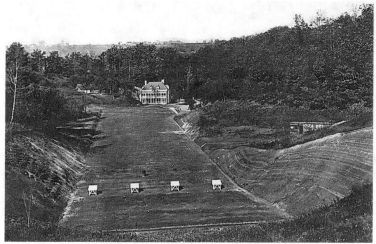

The rifle range and elegant clubhouse, circa 1930s.
(Photo courtesy of Joseph Schuler)

Genesee Valley Chapter of the Adirondack Mountain Club under the leadership of Dick Spade. They have been building and maintaining the trails here ever since. Most recently they worked with the Penfield Trails Committee to get trail easements across private property so the trail could be extended all the way to Ellison Park. The two new trail segments are:

Irondequoit Creek Wetlands - East Trail: 1.1 miles

Irondequoit Creek Wetlands - West Trail: 1.0 mile

You're in for a challenging, but beautiful hike. The trail winds up and down sharp hills and in and out gullies as it weaves through a maturing mixed wood forest. Giant tulip trees tower overhead with lush greenery on the forest floor below, including large patches of ferns and abundant poison ivy. In late spring the creek banks are awash in patches of yellow iris.

Trail Directions
• From the parking area, walk south toward a group of three large telephone poles on a narrow white-blazed trail, uphill through a field. As you start on the trail a private driveway to the Wetlands Center will be on your right.
• Enter the woods and pass a small trail to the left. (This side trail leads uphill to a panoramic view of Irondequoit Bay looking north and to a housing development looking south.) Follow white blazes as you continue straight.
• Cross a small foot bridge.
• Head downhill to the valley floor at 0.5 mile.
• Pass a small trail to the right leading to the Wetlands Center driveway.
• Pass a blue trail veering off to the right. Continue uphill on the white trail.
• Pass a blue and white-blazed trail on the right.
• Pass a blue trail to the right.

Before it spills into Irondequoit Bay, Irondequoit Creek wiggles through a broad wetland lined with cattails.

- At 1 mile pass a yellow-blazed trail to the left. (This will be part of the return loop.) Continue straight on the white-blazed trail.
- Pass a white & yellow-blazed trail on the left. Turn right following the white blazes.
- Emerge to a small clearing and reach an intersection. (You're now in the old rifle range. To your right is the old road entrance; now private property.) Continue straight.
- Climb a flight of cement stairs and pass under the new gazebo.
- Pass a red trail on your right, continue straight on white.
- Pass another red trail on your right. Continue straight.
- Pass a salmon-blazed trail on the left.
- Pass a pink trail on the right. Pass the pink trail on the right again. Continue straight.
- At 1.4 mile, begin descending the hill.
- The white trail turns hard left. Straight goes to Irondequoit Creek and the area known as "The Narrows" with a man-made dam. After viewing the creek turn around and return to the white trail turning right and following the edge of the creek.
- Step over a notched log. Reach the junction of several small trails. Turn a sharp left and head uphill, following the white trail.
- Pass an unmarked trail on the right, then the yellow trail on the right. Follow the white-blazed trail uphill.
- Pass the salmon trail twice, then an unmarked trail, all on your left.
- Turn left onto the yellow trail. The white trail veers off and becomes the Irondequoit Creek Wetlands Trail, leading to the parking area at the end of Old Browncroft Blvd. Straight heads to private homes.
- A yellow & white trail enters from the left. Continue on yellow uphill.
- At 2.3 miles you'll be back in the rifle range area near a cement trough with machinery that used to run the targets and a protective bunker for the target operator.

- Pass an unmarked trail to the left of the bunker. Continue following the yellow trail.
- At 2.6 miles, meet the white-blazed trail and turn right (N) to head uphill.
- Follow white blazes back to the parking area.

Date Hiked: _____

Notes:

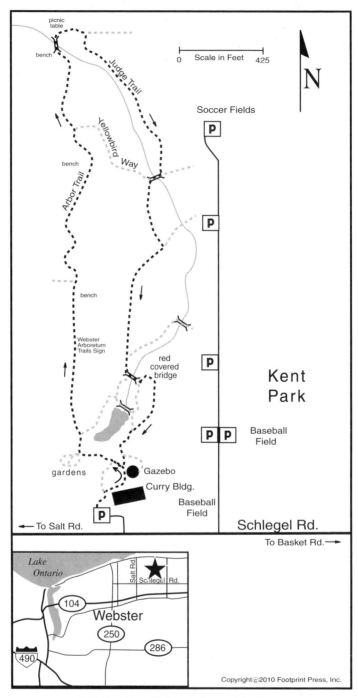

Webster Arboretum Trail

53

Webster Arboretum

Location:	Kent Park on Schlegel Road, Webster
Directions:	From Rochester, take Route 104 east through Webster. Turn north on Salt Road and east on Schlegel Road. The parking area is on the north side of Schlegel Road.
Alternative Parking:	Parking at the athletic fields of Kent Park
Hiking Time:	30 minutes
Length:	0.9 mile loop
Difficulty:	👣 👣 👣 👣
Surface:	Mowed-grass and dirt trail
Trail Markings:	None
Uses:	🚶 🎿
Dogs:	OK on leash
Admission:	Free
Contact:	The Webster Arboretum Association, Inc. PO Box 782, Webster, NY 14580-0782 http://websterarboretum.org

Webster Arboretum is a 32-acre segment of the 84.5-acre Kent Park. Gardener Elizabeth Sykes and local garden clubs had long envisioned a unique garden of natural beauty, which would draw people for leisure, educational, and cultural activities. Finally, during the 150th year town celebrations, Webster supervisor Adrian Stanton had the arboretum land set aside, and Parks Director Donna Fauth was assigned to develop the park. George Turner, chairman of the Webster Conservation Board recruited Elmer Smith, Mike Kopicki, and Dick Finicchia to work on the arboretum design. Elizabeth's 20-year dream is being brought to reality through private donations coordinated by the Webster Arboretum Association, Inc., a not-for-profit charitable organization.

Upon leaving the parking area, the first thing a visitor notices are the gardens. Volunteers from the five Webster Garden Clubs have built the Smith Rose Garden and a series of perennial gardens. They're designed to attract humming birds, butterflies, and the awe of human visitors with splashes of brilliant color. Next to the gardens sits the Norman R. Curry building with a multi-purpose room and restrooms.

According to Webster's dictionary, an arboretum is a place where many kinds of trees and shrubs are grown for exhibition and study. Beyond the gardens of the

The gardens and Curry building at Webster Arboretum.

Webster Arboretum, a trail leads past a pond, into the trees and shrubs available for your study. Benches are found periodically along the wide trail, inviting you to sit and savor your surroundings.

Trail Directions
• Head behind the Curry Building and follow the red brick path to the large gazebo.
• Turn left in front of the gazebo onto the gravel path. The pond will be on your right.
• Pass a gravel path with a small arbor on your left.
• Leave the gravel path and head left (S) toward the "Arboretum Trails" sign. (Note: you will not be able to see the sign until you pass through the pine trees.)
• Pass underneath the trail sign.
• Pass a bench.
• Cross a swamp area on a boardwalk.
• Pass "Yellowbird Way" on the right.
• Enter into a deep forest and pass a bench.
• Cross a bridge over a creek.
• Turn right on the Judge Trail. Straight goes to ball playing fields.
• A creek is now on the right.
• Bear right across a bridge. Left goes to a parking lot.
• After crossing the bridge, turn left at the "T." Right is the Yellowbird Way.
• Come to a "T," turn right. Left goes to a parking lot.
• Continue straight into an old apple orchard.
• Head across the grass toward the red covered bridge.
• You're now on a gravel path. At the "T," turn left. Right goes over another bridge and back to the beginning.
• Pass a drinking fountain and then a gravel path on the left.
• Pass a large gazebo on your left. You're now on a brick path.
• Continue to an arbor and back to the parking lot.

Leslie Huey chooses a beautiful rest spot along the trails at Webster Arboretum.

Date Hiked: _____

Notes:

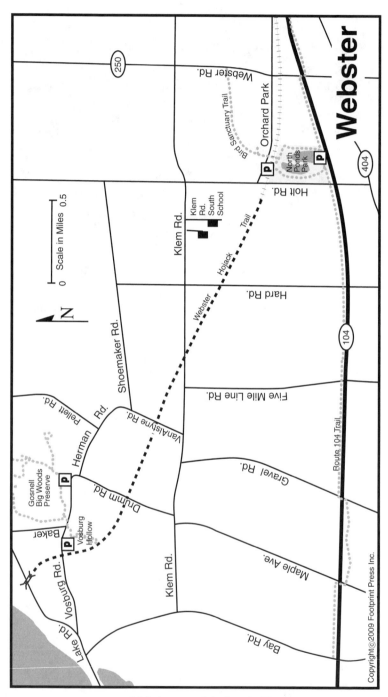

Webster Hojack Trail

54

Webster Hojack Trail

Location:	Between Lake Road and North Ponds Park, Webster
Directions:	From Route 104, head north on Bay Road. At the end, turn right onto Lake Road then right again onto Vosburg Road. Pass under the old railroad bridge (now part of Webster Hojack Trail) and watch right for the Vosburg Hollow parking area. Hikers can follow the trail through Vosburg Hollow to reach the Webster Hojack Trail. (See the Gosnell Big Woods Preserve Map on page 221 for more detail.) Bikers should head west on Vosburg Road and pick up the Webster Hojack Trail where it crosses Vosburg Road.
Alternative Parking:	There is room to pull off the road at any of the road intersections.
Hiking Time:	2 hours round trip
Length:	6.8 miles round trip
Difficulty:	🥾🥾
Surface:	Grass and cinder path
Trail Markings:	None
Uses:	🚶 🚴 🐎 🎿
Dogs:	OK
Admission:	Free
Contact:	Friends of Webster Trails Webster Community Center 985 Ebner Drive, Webster, NY 14580 www.webstertrails.org

Webster Hojack Trail is a rail-trail. In the 1850s the farmers of Webster had three options for shipping their produce to market. They could endure an all-day wagon ride to Rochester, an eight-mile wagon ride to the Erie Canal in Fairport, or meet a schooner at Nine Mile Point on Lake Ontario. All were arduous choices.

The prominent businessmen of Webster worked with representatives from other towns between Lewiston and Oswego to inspire the creation of the Lake Ontario Shore Railroad Company in 1868. In 1876 trains began arriving and departing from the Webster station. The line was sold to the Rome, Watertown and Ogdensburg Railroad and the abbreviations R.W. & O.R.R. became known as "Rotten Wood and Old Rusty Rails."

In 1889 a major crash occurred as a westbound train from the Thousand Islands rammed a train as it boarded passengers bound for Rochester. Many Webster homes became temporary hospitals to care for the injured. This crash brought about the use of automotive brakes on railroads.

The Webster train station became a hub of activity. In the fall, the railroad was hard pressed to supply enough cars to transport all the apples from local orchards. The Basket Factory was built along the tracks and became the largest and most productive basket factory in the world. Companies such as the Webster Canning and Preserving Company (a predecessor to Curtice-Burns), the Basket Factory, John W. Hallauer and Sons Evaporated Fruits, Martin Brothers Lumber Company, Webster Lumber Company, and LeFrois Pickling Factory, all owed their existence to the railroad.

The Lake Ontario Shore Railroad became known as the Hojack Line when a nameless farmer's mule-drawn buckboard stopped halfway across the tracks when a train was coming. The framer shouted "Ho Jack! Ho Jack!" to get his mule to move. The amused trainmen picked up on it and the name stuck.

This rail line, like all others in the area, was doomed by the increase in trucks and automobiles. Thanks to the Friends of Webster Trails it became a hiking and biking trail in 1997. To read more about the history of this rail line and the Hojack Station, check the Friends of Webster Trails web site.

For a short walk, the most scenic section is the 0.9-mile stretch from Drumm Road to Vosburg Road. At first cliffs tower above you, then the trail follows a raised bed high above the surrounding countryside. You can make it into a loop using the beautiful walk down into Vosburg Hollow. Leave the rail-trail shortly before Vosburg Road to wander downhill and cross Shipbuilders Creek on a bridge. Then follow Vosburg Road west to pick up the Hojack Trail again.

Trail Directions
- From the Vosburg Hollow parking lot, walkers can follow the Vosburg Hollow trail to reach the Webster Hojack trail. Bikers or those preferring a more level route can go west on Vosburg Road.
  Option 1: (Hiking through Vosburg Hollow to the Hojack Trail)
  Take the wooden steps that lead downhill to a bridge over Shipbuilders Creek. On the other side of the creek, bear right, then bear left at the next junction to follow the red-blazed trail away from the creek.
  Head uphill through the hollow until you reach the 8-foot-wide Webster Hojack Trail. Turn right to walk to the dead-end at Lake Road, or left for the longer segment.
  Option 2: (Short road walk to the Hojack Trail)
  Walk or ride back to Vosburg Hollow Road and turn left. Follow the road a short distance to the 8-foot-wide Webster Hojack Trail crossing. Turn right to walk to the dead-end at Lake Road, or left for the longer segment.
  Note: Entering the trail, heading south from Vosburg Road, you'll see an intimidating sign stating "no motorized vehicles." This northern segment of trail is

used as a driveway for a few homes. It is OK to hike or bike this portion of trail past the houses.

If you head right (northwest):
• Cross Vosburg Road.
• The trail ends after the bridge over Lake Road, marked by two large boulders. (A small path leads downhill to Lake Road, but no parking is available here.) Turn around and retrace your path.

If you head left (southeast):
• Pass a yellow metal trail barricade and cross Drumm Road diagonally to the right.
• Pass an old cement railroad post inscribed "P87," denoting 87 miles to Pulaski. Pulaski must have been a major port into Lake Ontario in the heyday of the railroads.
• Cross VanAlstyne Road.
• Reach Klem Road. Cross diagonally toward the right.
• On your right, watch for the cement pillar with a "W," telling the train's engineer to blow the whistle.
• Cross Hard Road.
• At the dead-end, turn around and retrace your path. (The trail is not cleared to Holt Road.)

Date Hiked: _____
Notes:

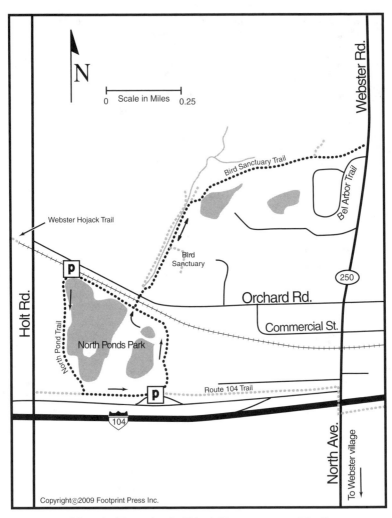

North Ponds & Bird Sanctuary Trails

55

North Ponds & Bird Sanctuary Trails

Location:	North Ponds Park, Webster
Directions:	From Route 104, head north on Webster Road (Route 250) and turn left (W) onto Orchard Road. The free parking lot is on the left before Holt Road.
Alternative Parking:	Off the westbound Route 104 entrance ramp, off Route 250 - pay in summer (June 13 through August 31), free the rest of the year
Hiking Time:	1 hour for North Ponds and Bird Sanctuary Trails
Length:	1.1-mile loop around North Ponds Park
	Bird Sanctuary Trail is 0.8 mile long
	2.7 miles total hike
Difficulty:	👣 👣
Surface:	Paved path in North Ponds Park, Bird Sanctuary Trails is a combination mowed grass and dirt path
Trail Markings:	None
Uses:	(North Ponds Park Trail only)
Dogs:	OK on leash
Admission:	Free
Contact:	Webster Parks and Recreation Department
	985 Ebner Drive, Webster, NY 14580
	(585) 872-2911
	http://websterparksandrecreation.org/index.php#
	Friends of Webster Trails
	Webster Community Center
	985 Ebner Drive, Webster, NY 14580
	www.webstertrails.org

North Ponds Park used to be a popular swimming area. Swimming is no longer allowed. An easy, paved trail with 8 handicapped fitness stations circumnavigates the park's two largest ponds and makes a nice walk, run or skate surface. Picnic shelters are available. In 2006, a sledding hill was added at the north end of the park. The area can be somewhat noisy from traffic on nearby Route 104.

The Bird Sanctuary Trail arches northeast from North Ponds Park, through a mature mixed forest with an open understory. It's a quiet walk until just before its end at Route 250.

Trail Directions
- From the parking lot on Orchard Road, follow the path into North Ponds Park.
- At the "Y" junction bear right.
- Follow the path, bearing left as it winds around the ponds, past the picnic pavilion, restrooms, etc.
- Turn left after the Route 104 parking area.
- Watch for a small dirt path to the right and turn right to cross the railroad tracks and Orchard Road. (Walk toward the Bird Sanctuary Trail sign.)
- At the sign, bear right. (The trail to the left crosses to the other side of the creek and dead-ends shortly.)
- A large sign showing birds, marks a trail to the right. It leads to the bird sanctuary area with a bench and lots of bird houses in the trees.
- Pass several benches and a pond.
- Trails off to the left lead to private homes.
- The trail dead-ends at Route 250 (Webster Road). Turn around & walk back to the North Ponds Park Trail.
- Cross Orchard Road.
- Turn right onto the paved path.
- Turn right when you see the dirt path, to return to the Orchard Road parking lot.

Date Hiked: _____

Notes:

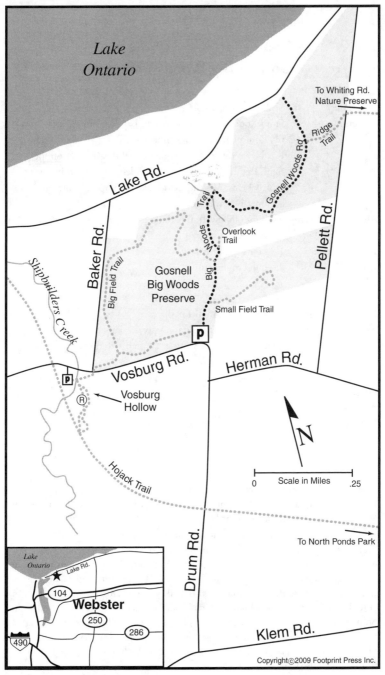

Gosnell Big Woods Preserve

56

Gosnell Big Woods Preserve

Location:	Vosburg Road, Webster
Directions:	From Route 104, head north on Bay Road to the end. Turn right onto Lake Road, then take the first right onto Vosburg Road. Pass the Vosburg Hollow Trail parking area on the right. Pass Baker Road and watch left for the parking area shortly before Vosburg Road takes a sharp right turn and becomes Drum Road.
Alternative Parking:	Vosburg Hollow Trail parking lot, marked by a sign along Vosburg Road, west of Baker Road.
Hiking Time:	1.5 hours round trip
Length:	2.4 miles round trip
Difficulty:	🥾 🥾
Surface:	Mowed-grass and dirt paths
Trail Markings:	Wooden trail name signs on posts at junctions (colored dot blazes on trees are graffiti and may be removed)
Uses:	🚶 🎿
Dogs:	OK on leash
Admission:	Free
Contact:	Friends of Webster Trails Webster Community Center 985 Ebner Drive, Webster, NY 14580 www.webstertrails.org

In 2006 the Town of Webster was able to preserve the old growth forest of Gosnell Big Woods Preserve through the generosity of Thomas & Georgia Gosnell and partnerships with the Trust for Public Land and the Genesee Land Trust.

Big Woods Trail, Gosnell Woods Road (which is a trail, not a road) and Ridge Trail wind on and off glacial eskers through a shady mixture of young and old-growth forests of beech, maple, oak, birch and pine. The Big Field Loop Trail is an easier, level walk around the perimeter of a field where bluebird boxes can be found. From the southwest corner of this trail, you can cross Vosburg Road and enter the trails of Vosburg Hollow, which in turn connect to the Hojack Rail Trail. Shipbuilders Creek flows through the valley at Vosburg Hollow, passing through a culvert under the old Lake Ontario Shore Railroad (Hojack Line) which is now the Hojack Trail (see page #214). From the creek, the trails climb through a pine forest to reach the raised rail bed.

Distances:

Big Field Trail Loop: 1.3-mile loop

Big Woods Trail & Gosnell Woods Road: 2.4 miles round trip

From the Gosnell Big Woods Preserve parking area to the Hojack Trail through Vosburg Hollow : 1.0 mile round trip

Trail Directions

• From the parking lot at the corner of Vosburg and Drum Roads, pass through the split rail fence.

• Continue straight (N) on the Big Woods Trail. (A left is the Big Field Trail.)

• Pass the Small Field Trail to the right, then the intersection of the Big Field Trail to the left.

• At the next junction, continuing straight will take you to the dead-end overlook for a short side trip. Turn left to stay on the Big Woods Trail. (This is the old-growth section of the forest.)

• Cross a wooden bridge over a creek, then climb a hill.

• Bear right at the next "Y." (The trail to the left dead-ends shortly in a swampy area.)

• Follow the main trail along the esker ridge.

Signs point the way at
Gosnell Big Woods Preserve.

• At the top of a hill, bear left to take Gosnell Woods Road.

• Pass the Ridge Trail to the right. (This can extend your hike as a side trail. It leads to the Whiting Road Nature Preserve.)

• Reach the end of Gosnell Woods Road marked by a "end of trail" sign and turn around. (A small trail continues straight to Lake Road but it traverses private property.)

• Follow the trail back to the parking lot. (Take a right on the Big Field trail if you'd like to extend your hike.)

Date Hiked: _____

Notes:

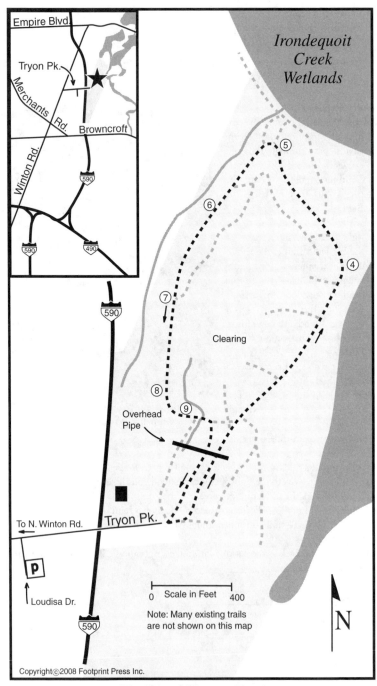

Empire Blvd.

Tryon Pk.

Merchants Rd.

Browncroft

Winton Rd.

590

590

490

Irondequoit Creek Wetlands

⑤

⑥

④

⑦

Clearing

⑧

⑨

Overhead Pipe

590

To N. Winton Rd.

Tryon Pk.

P

Loudisa Dr.

590

0   Scale in Feet   400

Note: Many existing trails
are not shown on this map

N

Copyright©2008 Footprint Press Inc.

Trails of Tryon Park

Revised Map of Tryon Park

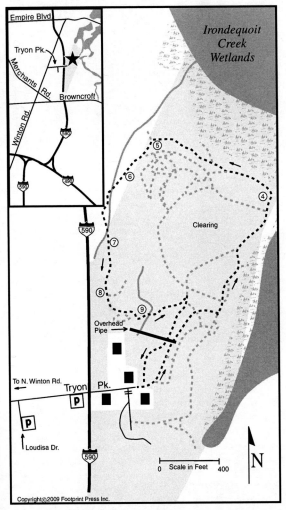

Trails of Tryon Park

Trails of Tryon Park

Location:	Tryon Park, Rochester
Directions:	From North Winton Road, turn west onto Tryon Park Road.
	Park on Tryon Park Road before the Interstate 590 overpass.
	Do not park between Interstate 590 and the trailhead.

Alternative Parking: At the end of Loudisa Drive in the baseball field parking area.

Hiking Time:	1 hour
Length:	1.4 mile loop
Difficulty:	👣 👣 👣
Surface:	Paved path and dirt trails
Trail Markings:	White blazes and numbers on trees
Uses:	🚶
Dogs:	OK on leash
Admission:	Free
Contact:	Monroe County Parks Department
	171 Reservoir Avenue, Rochester, NY 14620
	(585) 256-4950
	www.monroecounty.gov/parks-tryon.php

Tryon Park, or "deep Tryon" as it is known locally, is a hilly wooded, 80-acre urban oasis dedicated in 1971. It's a delightful walk through mature woods with views of Irondequoit Bay. The noise of Interstate 590 reminds you that civilization isn't far away. The park is on the site of the city's old sewage plant, but all that remains is an above-ground delivery pipe. Try this trail when leaves are off the trees for the best panoramic views of the creek waters winding their way through cattail wetlands at the southern end of Irondequoit Bay.

The loop described here is occasionally white-blazed, with numerical markers on the trees along the west side of the loop. It starts on high ground, dips down to water level, then climbs back to a ridge as it loops back to Tryon Park Road. The adventurous can spend many hours hiking all the trails in this park.

Although bicycling is currently illegal in this park (as in all Monroe County Parks), watch out for mountain bikers who frequently use the trails. As of 2010, Monroe County Parks is evaluating legalizing biking here.

Unfortunately, parts of the trail are a magnet for litter, and we encourage hikers to help out by taking along a small trash bag and picking up litter as they hike.

Trail Directions

- At end of Tryon Park Road, pass a yellow gate and bear left, heading downhill. (Straight ahead, another trail goes uphill. You won't notice the first trail to the left, it's hidden by trees.)
- Pass under the old sewage delivery pipe. Although the trail is a paved path, it is in disrepair, so watch your footing!
- At the "T," turn left, staying on the paved path.
- You quickly come to a "Y." Bear right. You are now going downhill on a dirt path, with a sharp drop-off on your right.
- Shortly after the trail levels off, at 0.4 miles, bear right (N) at a "Y" and head into the forest, approaching the wetlands.
- At 0.5 miles, you will pass a tree with 5 on it. The wetlands will open up in front of you, with the bay as a backdrop.
- The trail bears right. You now have the wetlands and bay to your right.
- As you begin to head uphill, pass a tree marked with a 6.
- At the top of the hill, bear left, away from the wetlands.
- The trail heads steeply uphill, with a gully on your right.
- Immediately after passing a tree marked 8, the trail turns left, going away from I-590 and emerging into a small clearing. Keep to the left and look for the white blazes to keep you on the right path.
- After heading downhill, bear right and cross a dry stream bed.
- At 1.3 miles, turn right and head uphill.
- Continue along the path that was once a stream bed, passing under the pipeline.
- Continue uphill to Tryon Park Road.

Date Hiked: _____

Notes:

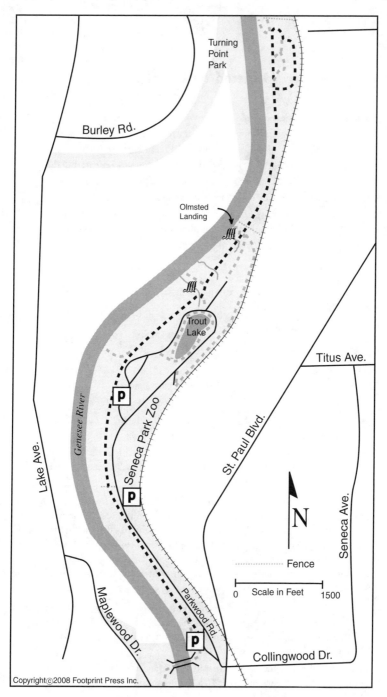

Turning
Point
Park

Burley Rd.

Olmsted
Landing

Trout
Lake

Genesee River

Seneca Park Zoo

Lake Ave.

Titus Ave.

St. Paul Blvd.

Seneca Ave.

N

.... Fence

Scale in Feet

0   1500

Maplewood Dr.

Parkwood Rd.

Collingwood Dr.

Olmsted/Seneca Trail

58

Olmsted/Seneca Trail

Location:	Seneca Park on Parkwood Road, Rochester
Directions:	From Route 104, exit north onto St. Paul Boulevard. Turn east onto Parkwood Road toward the Seneca Park Zoo. Park at the first car turn around after entering the park, near the Monroe County Pure Waters bridge.
Alternative Parking:	Several spots along Parkwood Road, in the zoo parking lot, or along the road as it circles Trout Lake.
Hiking Time:	2.5 hours minimum (without side trips into the gorge)
Length:	4.3 miles round trip
Difficulty:	🥾 🥾 🥾
Surface:	Woodchip path, gravel path
Trail Markings:	None
Uses:	🚶
Dogs:	OK on leash
Admission:	Free
Contact:	Monroe County Parks Department 171 Reservoir Avenue, Rochester, NY 14620 (585) 256-4950

The 297-acre Seneca Park was designed by Frederick Law Olmsted who is considered to be the founder of landscape architecture. He was prolific in the Rochester area where he designed four major parks: Seneca, Genesee Valley, Highland, and Maplewood.

Olmsted's designs were revolutionary for the late 1800s. Instead of laying out precise squares and gardens, he planned clumps of woods, meandering trails, bridle paths and spectacular views. He planted trees carefully to effect a "forested" look. This natural, quiet look was half of Olmsted's design philosophy. The other half created spaces for more active use, such as the open areas for ball fields and ponds for swimming in summer and ice skating in winter. Pavilions and bridges were designed in a neo-classic style to separate activity areas.

"A park should be accessible to the poor as well as the rich. It should be the beauty of the fields, the meadows, the prairies of green pastures, and the still waters. What we want to gain is tranquility and rest to the mind."
Frederick Law Olmsted

In its days of grandeur, swan boats plied back and forth taking passengers for a ride on Trout Lake. The boats carried 15 to 20 passengers on bench seats while the driver sat on a cast iron seat between two 4 foot high swans and peddled the pontoon boat. Today a paved path and picnic tables encircle the lake. The park is also home to the Seneca Park Zoo.

The Olmsted/Seneca Trail runs parallel to the steep Genesee River gorge. While there are no blazes, the trail is well defined and up to eight feet wide at times. Along the trail are dock access trails leading to the river's edge. Hiking down reveals the 400 million years of geologic history in the gorge walls and some waterfalls. (To view other area waterfalls pick up the guidebook *200 Waterfalls in Central & Western New York - A Finders' Guide*.) On the trail you pass wetlands, a pond, and many beautiful scenic views of the river. If you continue north the trail ends at Rattlesnake Point on top of the gorge cliff.

The Monroe County Pure Waters bridge was built in 1988. The 670 foot pedestrian bridge gives an excellent view of the surrounding gorge and river 100 feet below. It connects to the Genesee River Trail #4 (page 28) on the west bank of the river.

Trail Directions
- From the parking area near the Monroe County Pure Waters bridge, head northwest on the wide mulched trail with the Genesee River to your left.
- Pass a ramp entrance to the bridge.
- Pass the zoo parking lot.
- Follow the trail down to the fence opening on the left (at 0.5 mile) which was made to allow hikers only, and skinny ones at that, to pass through.
- Begin an easy descent on the wood chip path. Because the trail is in a park, there are many side trails off to the right. Stay on the main trail always heading north, staying near the river gorge.
- At 0.8 mile, pass the first trail into the gorge on the left.
- Pass restrooms.
- Trout Lake will appear to the right.
- At 1.1 miles, pass your first lookout. This is a nice place to sit at the bench and enjoy the view.
- At the "Y," bear right and cross a small bridge over a stream. (To the left is a small picnic/viewing area.)
- Bear left immediately after the bridge.
- Proceed gradually downhill, crossing two wooden bridges.
- At 1.2 miles, immediately after the second bridge, a trail to the left goes down to a dock on the Genesee River. This is the second side trail you'll have the chance to take, if you want to.
- Pass additional views with benches.
- At 1.4 miles, cross a small creek on a wooden bridge.
- Bear right at the fork, just before the second rise. (The trail to left with a split rail fence leads down 0.1 mile to a river dock and a waterfall view. This is called Olmsted Landing after Frederick Law Olmsted, the park's designer.)
- The trail now meets a gravel park access road. Follow the road, continuing to bear left (N) through a 10 foot high fence gate at 1.5 miles.

- Follow the old maintenance access road. (This is the narrowest part of the park with the gorge on the left and an abandoned railroad bed and private homes on the right.)
- At 1.8 miles, pass a gated access road on the right used by the park for composting.
- At the top of the next hill, turn right (SE) at the small side trail marked with orange diamond markers. You're heading away from the river gorge.
- Continue straight through a small trail intersection.
- At 2.1 miles, reach a "T," turn right again and bear left past the locked Seneca Road entrance (locked to vehicles, open to pedestrians).
- Follow the trail around to the left leading back to the gorge.
- Reach a four-way intersection at the edge of the gorge. (This is the farthest point north for the trail. Across the gorge is Turning Point Park - Trail #60 (page 235). One of the two trails on the right leads to the river and a dock. The other continues heading north to the end of county property and a gate.) Bear left and begin your return trip heading south along the gorge.
- Follow the edge of the gorge back to the gravel access road.
- At 2.4 miles, turn right (S) and follow the access road until you pass the open fence gate.
- Immediately watch for the trail on the right and turn right to stay near the gorge.
- At this point you will be retracing your steps back to where you began. Remember to stay on the trail nearest the gorge.

Date Hiked: _____

Notes:

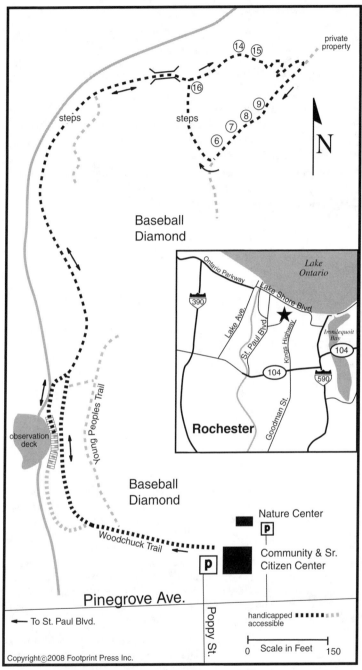

private property

⑭ ⑮

⑯

⑨
⑧
⑦
⑥

steps

steps

N

Baseball
Diamond

Lake
Ontario

Ontario Parkway

Lake Shore Blvd.

390

Lake Ave.

St. Paul Blvd.

Kings Highway

Irondequoit
Bay

104

104

590

Goodman St.

Rochester

Young Peoples Trail

observation
deck

Baseball
Diamond

Nature Center
P

Woodchuck Trail

P

Community & Sr.
Citizen Center

Pinegrove Ave.

◄— To St. Paul Blvd.

Poppy St.

handicapped ■■■■■■
accessible

0   Scale in Feet   150

Helmer Nature Center Trails

Helmer Nature Center Trails

Location:	Pinegrove Avenue, Irondequoit
Directions:	From Route 104, head north on St. Paul Boulevard. Turn east on Pine Grove Avenue. The Helmer Nature Center parking lot will be on the left (N).
Alternative Parking:	A driveway past the Nature Center. Drive to the far end and park on the left.
Hiking Time:	20 minutes (handicapped accessible loop)
	45 minutes (longer loop)
Length:	0.5 mile loop (handicapped accessible loop)
	1.2 mile loop (longer loop)
Difficulty:	🥾🥾 (handicapped accessible loop)
	🥾🥾🥾 (longer loop)
Surface:	Gravel and wood chip path
Trail Markings:	Some numbered posts
Uses:	🚶 ♿
Dogs:	Pets are NOT allowed
Admission:	Free
Contact:	Helmer Nature Center
	154 Pinegrove Avenue
	Rochester, NY 14617
	(585) 336-3035

The Helmer Nature Center began operation in 1973 under the West Irondequoit School District. The center utilizes the natural world as a classroom, providing learning opportunities, encouraging environmental awareness, and fostering the concept of global stewardship. They offer a wide range of both educational and community activities. Classes are offered on such diverse subjects as nature awareness, animal habitats, snowshoeing, Native American culture, pioneer living, outdoor cooking, and field studies. In addition, numerous festivals, open houses, and family programs are held, including the ever popular Maple Sugar Open House. After enjoying the trails, stop in the nature center to find out about upcoming events and consider becoming a member.

As the times change, so too does the landscape encompassed by the Helmer Nature Center. What was once vineyards and a vegetable or "truck" farm (named for the method used to transport the farm's produce to customers) is now a series of trails designed for use by all members of the community, including an ADA approved handicapped accessible loop leading down to the pond and observation deck.

Both loops described below have the same start and finish point, but the longer loop extends your hike into sections of the Nature Center that are not handicapped accessible.

Trail Directions (both loops):
- From the parking area, head left (W) on a gravel path behind the baseball diamond. (The wood chip path serves as the return route for the easy loop).
- Bear left, staying on the main trail as the Young People's Trail branches off to the right.
- The path heads down a long, relatively gentle slope, with a view of the pond below to the left.
- At the base of the hill (0.2 miles), take a hard left on the path to the pond. Gravel turns to boardwalk as you reach the pond and observation deck. This pond is a favorite for kids of all ages, so spend some time on the observation deck, and see how many different plants and animals you can identify in this habitat.

Handicapped Accessible Loop
- Take a right (S) when leaving the observation deck, and continue along the boardwalk.
- At the end of the boardwalk, the trail bears left and heads uphill on a wood chip path.
- The trail continues to twist and turn up the hill. Although somewhat steep, the trail is wheelchair navigable.
- Emerge at the top of the hill and continue straight (E) towards the parking lot.

Longer Loop
- Take a left (N) from the observation deck, retracing your steps along the boardwalk.
- Continue up the gravel path. The path merges with the main trail you took coming down the hill (the Woodchuck Trail, although it is not marked as such). You are now walking through a hilly, wooded section of the nature center.
- The trail turns from gravel to dirt; the path becomes somewhat uneven, and is no longer handicap accessible. Note the old vineyard terraces that cut through the hill on the right side of the path throughout this section.
- The trail goes downhill, with a few intermittent steps. A small wetland area separates the path from a creek.
- The path continues between the base of a hill, and a small creek on the left.
- Go up a few steps, then straight, past a trail on the right that heads uphill.
- Cross a wooden bridge.
- At post #16, continue straight on the wood lined path, past a trail to the right.
- As you pass post #15, the trail heads uphill, looping its way in a broad switchback up the former vineyard terraces.
- Take a right at the "T." Left, past the wooden frame, is private property.

- At 0.7 miles, turn right on a board-lined path. Going straight would lead out under a frame with a "Nature Trail" sign and along a thin path that runs between two athletic fields and ends at the parking lot.
- Head down stairs.
- At the "T" (post #16), take a left and cross the wooden bridge.
- Continue straight, passing a trail to the left.
- Pass a red bench on your left, and proceed uphill.
- At "Y," bear left and head uphill.
- Pass the Young People's Trail on the left. The trail comes out of woods behind the baseball diamond.
- Continue straight towards the parking lot.

Date Hiked: _____
Notes:

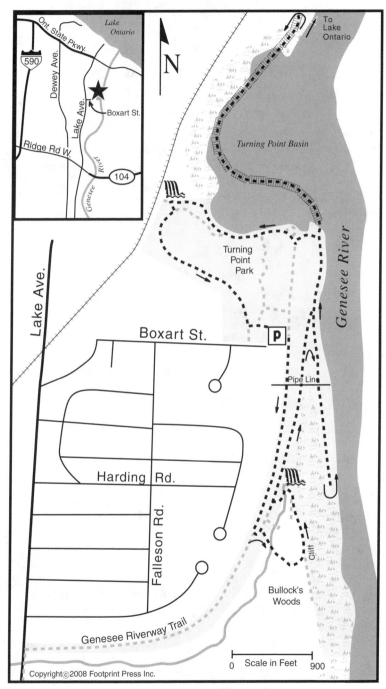

Copyright©2008 Footprint Press Inc.

Turning Point Park & Bullock's Woods Preserve

235

60

Turning Point Park & Bullock's Woods Preserve

Location:	Boxart Street, Charlotte
Directions:	From Lake Avenue (south of Stonewood Road), turn east on Boxart Street. The parking area is at the end of Boxart Street.
Alternative Parking:	None
Hiking Time:	2.5 hour loop
Length:	4.4 mile loop
Difficulty:	👣 👣 👣
Surface:	Dirt path, paved trail, boardwalk
Trail Markings:	None
Uses:	🚶 🎿
Dogs:	OK on leash
Admission:	Free
Contact:	Department of Parks, Recreation & Human Services City of Rochester 400 Dewey Avenue, Rochester, NY 14613 (585) 428-6770

Turning Point Park is a 112-acre wilderness setting in an urban environment. The term "Turning Point" has double meaning to the Charlotte residents nearby. Historically, the wide basin in the nearby Genesee River was a physical place that ships could turn around before encountering the Lower Falls. This was once a heavily used industrial area with ships visiting docks to load and unload coal, wheat, feldspar, paper boxes, and tourists. An active cement plant still operates on this site.

In 1972 the Rochester-Monroe County Port Authority announced plans to build an oil storage tank farm on the site. Area residents, led by Bill Davis, fought the plan which would have bulldozed a stand of 200-year-old oak trees and cut off community access to the river. They achieved a "turning point" in getting the city to turn away from commercial development of the river waterfront and toward its recreational use. The city bought the land in 1976 and opened Turning Point Park in 1977.

Another milestone came in 2006 when a winding boardwalk was built across Turning Point Basin and the trail was extended north 7.7 miles to Lake Ontario, as part of the Genesee Riverway Trail. (See trail #4, page 28.)

236

From the parking area, your journey will start high on a cliff with panoramic views of the river valley below. You'll walk a paved path, gradually downhill, then veer off for a loop through Bullock's Woods. Back to an old railroad grade, you'll continue downhill, passing a waterfall, until you reach river level. Walking along the river you'll pass a series of docks, both active and abandoned. Essroc Materials, Inc., Great Lakes Cement Division still uses these docks to unload dry cement to the large storage tanks which sit atop the cliff. Wander across Turning Point Basin on the boardwalk, then return to Turning Point Park.

After exploring the river's edge, you'll climb back uphill. Then loop through a forest with 200-year-old oak trees, passing another waterfall, before returning to the parking area. (To enjoy other area waterfalls, pick up a copy of *200 Waterfalls in Central & Western New York - A Finders' Guide*.) Thanks Bill Davis for having the foresight to save this urban treasure.

Cement gets pumped from cargo ships through
green pipes to storage tanks at the top of the cliff
in Turning Point Park.

The *Essroc* delivers cement to the docks at Turning Point Park for the Essroc Materials Company, Great Lakes Cement Division.

Trail Directions

- From the parking area, walk south on the paved walkway toward the "Turning Point Park" sign and overhead green pipes. This paved section of the trail is part of the Genesee Riverway Trail #4 (page 28).
- Pass under the green pipes. (They pump dry cement from ships at the dock to the large storage tanks.)
- At 0.3 mile, take a sharp left off the abandoned railbed, and double back on a paved trail just before some wooden posts.
- Take the first right and head downhill on a small dirt trail. (If you miss this, there are two more trails to the right that head downhill. Any of them will take you across a small creek, into Bullock's Woods.)
- Cross the small creek.
- Immediately, turn right (S).
- The trail circles left to a cliff overlooking the river. At 0.5 mile, turn left (N) to follow the cliff edge.
- Pass a trail to the right. (It leads to a dead-end near the base of the Bullock's Woods Waterfall.) (Note: this is one of the many local waterfalls you can visit using the guidebook *200 Waterfalls in Central & Western New York - A Finders' Guide.*)
- Reach a "T," and turn right. (Left circles back to where you originally crossed the small creek.)
- Cross the small creek and climb to the rail-trail.
- Turn right, back onto the rail-trail.
- At 0.9 mile, there used to be an observation deck to the right overlooking a waterfall. It's gone now, but you can still look over the cliff edge to glimpse Bullock's Woods Waterfall from above.
- Continue downhill and cross under the green pipes.
- Reach a "T" near water level. Turn right (S).

Walkers enjoy the new boardwalk over Turning Point Basin.

- Pass old docks to the left.
- This trail dead-ends at a cul-de-sac overlooking a cattail swamp area at 1.6 miles.
- Turn around and retrace your steps.
- Continue straight past the railtrail to the left and an old road to the left.
- To the right, steps allow you to walk (or launch a boat) down to water's edge.
- At 2.0 miles, pass through the yellow gates and walk out on the boardwalk which winds across Turning Point Basin. The old docking platforms now serve as observation decks.
- When you reach land again at 2.6 miles, turn around and return to Turning Point Park. (Continuing north on this trail takes you to Lake Ontario in Charlotte.)
- Take the first right (W), heading uphill.
- At the top of the hill, turn right (E) onto a dirt trail.
- Continue straight, past a small paved trail. (It leads to a lookout to the right.)
- Quickly pass through a small trail intersection.
- At the "Y," bear right (E).
- At 3.8 miles pass a paved path to the left.
- The trail bends left. (Straight ahead is the second waterfall (Red Falls) and a dead-end at active railroad tracks.) Take a sharp left turn onto a paved path.
- At 4.0 miles reach a "Y," and bear right (SW).
- At 4.3 miles turn left on a dirt path. (Straight ends at Boxart Street.)
- Bear right past a trail to the left and continue to the parking area.

Date Hiked: _____

Notes:

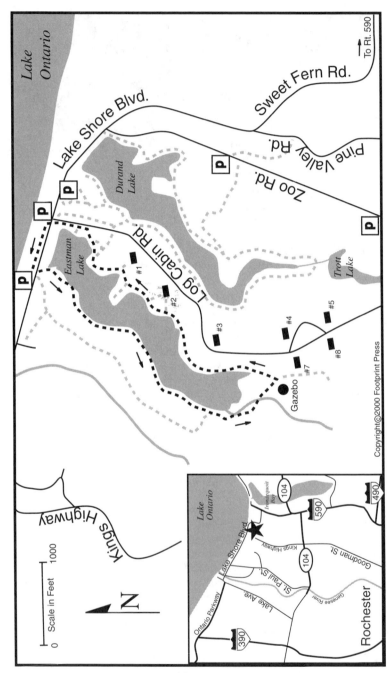

Eastman Lake Trail

61

Eastman Lake Trail

Location:	Durand Eastman Park, Rochester
Directions:	Durand Eastman Park can be found along the shore of Lake Ontario, east of the Genesee River. Park in the parking area between Lake Shore Boulevard and Lake Ontario, near the northwest corner of Eastman Lake, across from Log Cabin Road.
Alternative Parking:	Along Log Cabin Road in Durand Eastman Park
Hiking Time:	1 hour
Length:	1.8 mile loop
Difficulty:	🥾 🥾 🥾 🥾
Surface:	Dirt path
Trail Markings:	None
Uses:	🚶 🎿
Dogs:	OK on leash
Admission:	Free
Contact:	Monroe County Parks Department 171 Reservoir Avenue, Rochester, NY 14620 (585) 256-4950

Durand Eastman Park was a gift to the City of Rochester in 1908 from Dr. Henry Durand and George Eastman. This gave the city its first beachfront property and an opportunity for residents to explore the countryside outside the city's residential boundaries. Ownership passed to the County of Monroe in 1961.

Today the park is known mainly for its long sandy Lake Ontario beach, public golf course, and arboretum with herds of deer. During the winter the golf course becomes part of a network of cross-country ski trails. In summer, the trails are a bit more limited as golfers use their course. Still, a woods walk around Eastman Lake is a pleasure any time of year. It does require a 0.2 mile road walk to complete the loop. On the lake you'll often see herons, geese and swans.

Between the parking lots off Lake Shore Boulevard and Lake Ontario you'll now find the 4.8-mile-long paved Irondequoit Lakeside Trail. Built in 2007, this multi-use trail follows the old CSX railroad bed and offers great views of the lake year-round. Head toward the lake for a short stroll after you finish the Eastman Lake loop.

The trail around
Eastman Lake.

Trail Directions
- From the parking area, cross Lake Shore Boulevard heading southeast.
- Enter the woods at the northwest corner of Eastman Lake. (Not on the mowed-grass area directly across from the parking area.)
- Pass some small trails off the main trail. The lake will appear to your left. Continue west along the edge of Eastman Lake.
- At 0.4 mile, pass a trail to the right. Continue straight (SW).
- At 0.6 mile, pass a cement structure.
- Just before reaching the golf course (mowed-grass) turn left (S) to cross some corduroy in a low, wet area.
- Reach a small creek at 0.7 mile. Bear right and follow the trail to the golf course.
- Turn left (SW) and cross the creek on a culvert along the edge of the golf course.
- Walk south along the edge of the golf course toward the gazebo.
- Enter the woods (E) on a trail to the left of the gazebo.
- Reach a "T" with a wide trail and turn left (N).
- Stay on the main trail. Several small trails will head off on both sides.
- The lake is now to your left.
- Additional small trails will lead off. Continue on the main trail along the lake.
- Continue straight through a small trail intersection (left leads to the tip of a peninsula).
- At 1.4 miles, pass a trail to the right that leads uphill to Shelter #1.
- Notice the large patch of Rhododendron on the hill to your right.
- The main trail veers away from the lake. At 1.5 miles, turn right. (The trail left loops through a low wet area.)
- Head uphill to Log Cabin Road.
- Turn left (N) and follow the road toward Lake Ontario.
- At 1.7 mile, cross Lake Shore Boulevard. Turn left and follow the grass area along the road back to the parking area.

Date Hiked: _____

Notes:

Central
Section

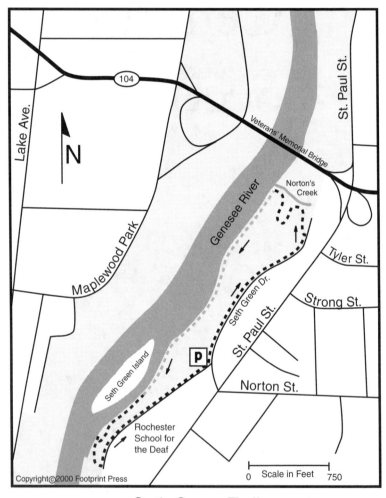

Seth Green Trail

62

Seth Green Trail

Location:	Seth Green Drive, Rochester
Directions:	From Route 104, exit south on St. Paul Boulevard. Turn west on Seth Green Drive. Take the first left to find the parking area.
Alternative Parking:	None
Hiking Time:	20 minutes round trip (official trail)
	40 minute loop (gorge loop trail)
Length:	0.9 mile round trip (official trail)
	1.4 mile loop (gorge loop trail)
Difficulty:	👣 👣 👣 👣
Surface:	Dirt path, paved road
Trail Markings:	None
Uses:	🚶
Dogs:	OK on leash
Admission:	Free
Contact:	Monroe County Parks Department
	171 Reservoir Avenue, Rochester, NY 14620
	(585) 256-4950

Two routes are described for the Seth Green Trail. The first is the official route which leads from the parking area to a switchbacked trail into the gorge and back out again. It follows a historic trail used by Native Americans for thousands of years. This trail offers a unique experience of the gorge as it descends past a dramatic rock face and waterfall below Seneca Towers and terminates at the river's edge.

The gorge loop trail uses maintained trails at either end of the loop but includes a 0.5-mile stretch of rough trail along the edge of the river which is nothing more than a path created by fishermen looking for a good casting spot. The loop is passable, but to follow it you have to expect some rough footing, downed trees, and overgrown bushes. It is easy to follow, with the river as your guide, but it is not a manicured trail. (This section is shown on the map as a grey trail.)

The land you'll walk is part of Seneca Park. The RG&E service road beyond the parking area leads to the base of the Lower Falls. In the early 1800s this area was home to the village of Carthage. It thrived as a steamboat landing and active mill site but was absorbed into Rochester upon its incorporation in 1834.

So, who was Seth Green? Adonijah Green ran a tavern at the corner of St. Paul and Norton Streets. His son Seth, born in 1817, spent many hours as a boy fishing, hunting, and trapping along the river. He observed the habits of fish. After running a successful fish and chowder business, he started the Caledonia Fish Hatchery. Seth Green received national and international fame as a fish grower and conservationist. The salmon stocked in the Genesee River today comes from the Caledonia Fish Hatchery.

Trail Directions — official trail (0.9 mile round trip)
• From the parking area, walk northeast along Seth Green Drive.
• In 0.2 mile, find a sign on the left that reads "This historic trail was used by Native Americans for thousands of years. Pioneer settlers expanded the trail and founded Carthage here in 1817." Turn left (W) and head downhill on the dirt trail.

The Veterans Memorial Bridge from within the Genesee River gorge.

• Follow the switchbacks downhill.
• View Norton's Creek waterfall at 0.3 mile. (To view other local waterfalls, pick up a copy of the guidebook *200 Waterfalls in Central & Western New York - A Finders' Guide*.)
• Continue downhill to water level at 0.4 mile. (This was once the site of Brewer's Landing.)
• To return, retrace your path uphill, then right along Seth Green Drive.

Trail Directions — gorge loop trail (1.4 mile loop)

Note: The gate at the far end of this loop is open from 6 AM to 7 PM daily. Do not begin this loop if it's after 6 PM. If you hear a loud siren or see flashing lights, do not proceed along the river's edge. This is a signal from the RG&E plant that means high water is fast approaching.

• From the parking area, walk northeast along Seth Green Drive.
• In 0.2 mile, find a sign on the left that reads "This historic trail was used by Native Americans for thousands of years. Pioneer settlers expanded the trail and founded Carthage here in 1817." Turn left (W) and head downhill on the dirt trail.
• Follow the switchbacks downhill.
• View Norton's Creek waterfall at 0.3 mile.
• Continue downhill to water level at 0.4 mile. (This was once the site of Brewer's Landing.)
• At river level, head left (SW) along the edge of the river. (For the next 0.5 mile the trail will be unmaintained.)
• Cross through a tire dumping ground.
• At 0.7 mile, pass an outflow drain.
• Continue along the river's edge through a rocky area. This requires some rock hopping.
• Pass Seth Green Island to the right.
• Pass a trail to the right and head uphill.
• At 1.1 mile, reach the paved RG&E service road and turn left, continuing uphill. (Notice the geologic layers in the bank to your right as you ascend.)

The Lower Falls of the Genesee River.

247

• Pass through the gate to the parking area. (The gate is open 6 AM to 7 PM daily.)

Date Hiked: _____

Notes:

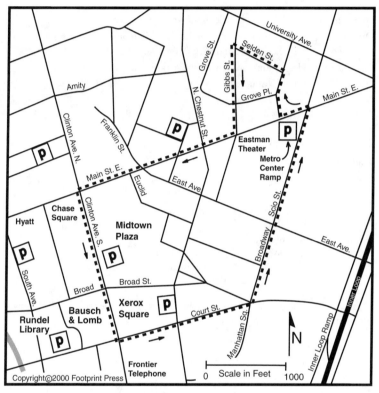

Grove Place Walk

63

Grove Place Walk

Location:	Theater District of downtown Rochester
Directions:	Exit the Inner Loop on East Main Street. Turn left on Scio Street and park in the Metro Center Ramp.
Alternative Parking:	Numerous downtown parking ramps
Hiking Time:	45 minutes
Length:	1.2 mile loop
Difficulty:	
Surface:	Sidewalks
Trail Markings:	Street signs
Uses:	
Dogs:	OK
Admission:	Free

Information Furnished by:
American Heart Association
2113 Chili Avenue, Rochester, NY 14624
(585) 426-4050

Enjoy a downtown stroll past quaint townhouses. Circle the remains of Midtown Plaza and Xerox Square on your tour of the best of downtown.

Trail Directions
- Exit the Metro Center Ramp Garage on Scio Street and head north.
- Turn left onto East Main Street.
- Pass Carpenter Alley then take a quick right (N) onto Windsor Street.
- Turn left (NW) at Selden Street and take another left (S) onto Gibbs Street.
- At 0.4 mile, reach East Main Street. Turn right (W).
- Walk five blocks, and turn left onto Clinton Avenue at 0.6 mile.
- In two blocks turn left onto Court Street.
- In another two blocks turn left onto Broadway.
- Continue straight as Broadway becomes Scio Street, and return to the Metro Center Ramp Garage.

Date Hiked: _____
Notes:

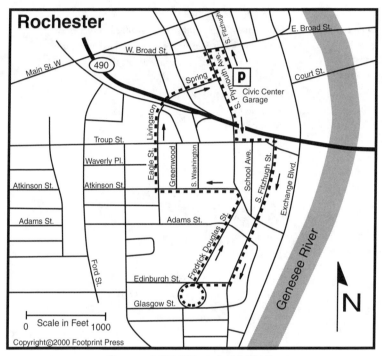

Corn Hill District Walk

64

Corn Hill District Walk

Location:	Corn Hill District of downtown Rochester
Directions:	From Interstate 490, take the Plymouth Street exit. From Plymouth Street turn east on Broad Street then enter the Civic Center Garage across from South Fitzhugh Street.
Alternative Parking:	Along the streets in Corn Hill
Hiking Time:	45 minutes
Length:	1.5 mile loop
Difficulty:	🥾 🥾
Surface:	Sidewalks
Trail Markings:	Street signs
Uses:	🚶 ♿
Dogs:	OK
Admission:	Free

Information Furnished by:
American Heart Association
2113 Chili Avenue, Rochester, NY 14624
(585) 426-4050

Step back in time as you wander through Corn Hill's neighborhood of restored homes. Before Nathaniel Rochester founded his name sake village in 1812, the Seneca Indians used this land for corn fields. Corn Hill was Rochester's first neighborhood, built in the early 1800s as flour milling boomed.

Today Corn Hill is a vibrant neighborhood of mansions and workers cottages, restored to their original splendor. Among the buildings you'll find examples of Greek and Gothic Revival, Italian Villa, Second Empire, and Queen Anne houses.

Trail Directions
• Exit the Civic Center Garage to Broad Street and turn left (W) on Broad Street.
• Turn left onto South Plymouth Avenue.
• Cross over Interstate 490 and turn left (E) at the first street, onto Troup Street.
• Bear right on Fitzhugh Street and pass the Landmark Society headquarters.
• Continue straight, past South Plymouth Avenue and Adams Street.
• At 0.7 mile, turn right (W) on Edinburgh Street.
• When you come to Frederick Douglas Street turn left and walk around the circle with the gazebo in the center.
• Continue west on Frederick Douglas Street after completing the circle.

One of many restored homes in the Corn Hill District.

- Continue straight through a small park.
- At 1.1 miles, turn left on South Plymouth Avenue.
- Turn left onto Atkinson Street.
- At 1.3 miles, turn right (N) on Eagle Street.
- Continue straight on Livingston Park.
- Head toward the pedestrian bridge over Interstate 490.
- Bear right on Spring Street.
- At 1.4 miles, turn left on South Plymouth Avenue.
- At Broad Street turn right and return to the Civic Center Garage.

Date Hiked: _____

Notes:

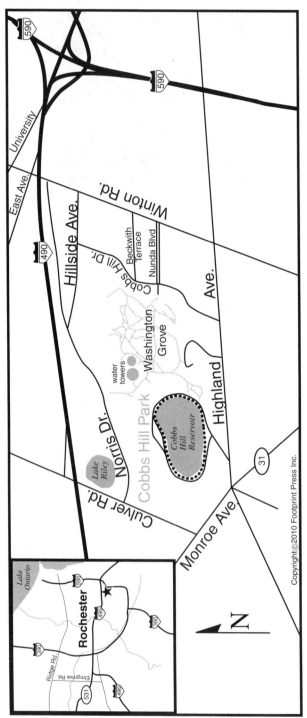

Reservoir Trail & Washington Grove

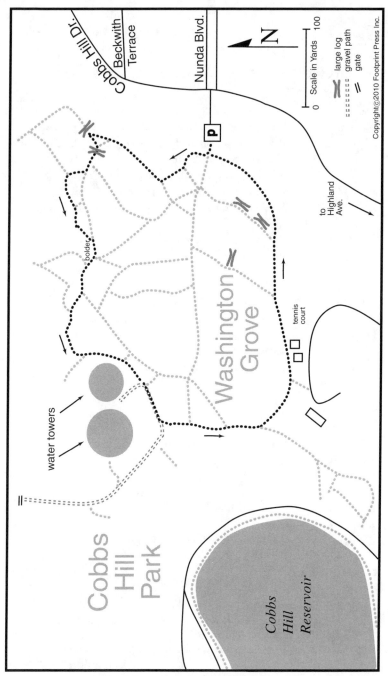

Washington Grove Trails

Reservoir Trail & Washington Grove Trail

Location:	Cobbs Hill Park, Rochester
Directions:	For Reservoir Trail: From Interstate 490, take the Culver Road exit and head south. Pass the entrance to lower Cobbs Hill Park (Norris Dr.). Turn left onto Monroe Ave. (Route 31), then take the first left onto Highland Ave. The first left will be an entrance into the upper part of Cobbs Hill Park. Follow the road uphill and follow the signs to park in legal spots.
Alternative Parking:	For Washington Grove Trail: Continue east on Highland Ave. & turn left onto Cobbs Hill Drive. Take the first left and park at the dead end of Nunda Blvd. to access Washington Grove.
Hiking Time:	25 minutes to circle the reservoir 30 minutes to hike Washington Grove
Length:	0.7 mile loop trail around the reservoir 0.8 mile loop in Washington Grove
Difficulty:	👣 👣 Washington Grove Trails 👣 Reservoir Trail
Surface:	Reservoir Trail is paved Washington Grove has dirt trails
Trail Markings:	None
Uses:	🚶 ♿ (only the Reservoir Trail is handicapped accessible)
Dogs:	OK on leash
Admission:	Free
Contact:	City of Rochester Bureau of Recreation 400 Dewey Ave., Rochester, NY 14613 (585) 428-6755 www.cityofrochester.gov/parks

Composed mostly of glacial deposits from about 12,000 years ago, Cobbs Hill is the beginning point of a set of hills (a recessional moraine) which run for a few miles and include Pinnacle Hill (the highest point in Rochester), Highland Park, and Mt. Hope Cemetery. (Mt. Hope Cemetery is a fascinating place to take a walk. For map & details pick up a copy of *Take Your Bike - Family Rides in the Rochester Area*.)

You'll find large trees and wide trails in Washington Grove.

In 1932, shortly after Rochester's reservoir was built, and Cobbs Hill Park was established (with a generous donation from George Eastman), the adjacent woodland called Washington (Memorial) Grove was dedicated as a memorial to the bicentennial of George Washington's birth. The grove was preserved to teach children the patriotic values associated with Washington and to teach the value of nature.

Today, Cobbs Hill Park has a lower and an upper section. Down low you'll find Lake Riley (good for fishing and ice skating) and sports fields. Lake Riley began life as a wide waters area along the Erie Canal back in the days when the Erie Canal looped through the heart of downtown Rochester. It's the upper section where you'll find the reservoir and Washington Grove.

The reservoir is encircled by a paved walking path and a road, with a panoramic view of the Rochester cityscape. A metal fence protects the reservoir. Nearby is the Water Board Building which resembles a Greek temple, where musicians often gather in summer. An easy stroll around the Reservoir Trail is not to be missed.

Next to the reservoir, Washington Grove is a 100 acre sanctuary of large oaks and an occasional rare American chestnut and butternut tree. It's home to two abandoned water towers and a maze of trails.

Over the years, the woodlands of Washington Grove became over loved (i.e. overused). In 2008 a coalition was formed, comprised of the Sierra Club, the City of Rochester, area residents, and interested volunteers to study and improve the conditions within Washington Grove. As a result of their study and on-going work, changes are being implemented to the vegetation and to the labyrinth of trails. Some trails are being abandoned, reclaimed and restored. This is still a work in progress, so follow any posted signs.

Washington Grove Trail Directions

- From the Nunda Blvd. parking area, enter the woods and take the first right at the notice board.
- A trail enters from the left. Bear right, heading downhill, then uphill.
- Bear right when a trail enters from the left again.
- Pass a trail on the left. Continue straight.
- Turn left before the log. Going across the log (straight) takes you downhill.
- Come to a "T." Turn right and step between the cut tree trunk.
- Pass a trail to the left.
- Bear right at the next "Y." Walk along the top of the hill with a drop off to the right.
- Pass a trail right going downhill to the right.
- A very small trail enters from the left. Continue straight.
- A trail enters from the left. Go straight, past a boulder.
- A trail enters from the left, bear right heading uphill.
- Pass a trail to the right that heads downhill.
- At the "Y," turn right, following the edge of the hill.
- Pass a trail to the right that goes downhill to Hillside School. Then bear left.
- A trail enters from the right. Continue straight.
- Continue walking the top edge of the hill up to and past the water tower.
- Pass a trail on the left. Continue straight.
- Continue straight, joining a large gravel trail at a 4-way intersection.
- At the "Y," bear left.
- Pass a side trail to the left. Continue straight.
- Pass another side trail to the left. Continue straight.
- Bear left at the "Y." Houses will now be on your right.
- Pass a trail to the right.
- Pass a tennis court to your right.
- Pass a trail to the left. Continue straight, walking between a large downed tree trunk.
- Pass another trail to the left. Continue straight along the edge of the hill heading downhill and back to the entrance.

Date Hiked: _____

Notes:

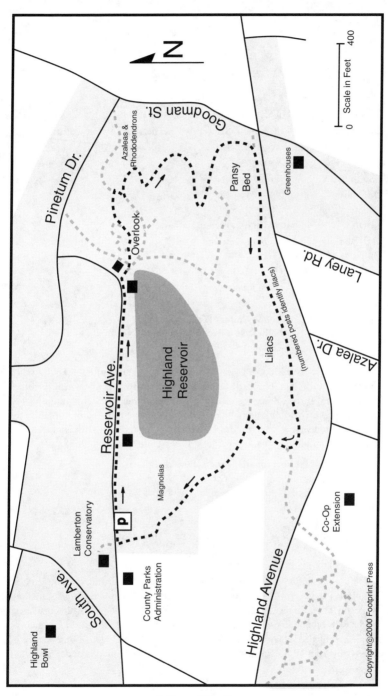

Lilac Trail

Map labels

N

Scale in Feet
0   400

Pinetum Dr.

Goodman St.

Azaleas & Rhododendrons

Pansy Bed

Greenhouses

Overlook

Laney Rd.

Reservoir Ave.

Highland Reservoir

Lilacs
(numbered posts identify lilacs)

Azalea Dr.

Magnolias

P

Lamberton Conservatory

South Ave.

County Parks Administration

Co-Op Extension

Highland Avenue

Highland Bowl

Lilac Trail

Location:	Highland Park, Rochester
Directions:	Park along Reservoir Avenue, near Lamberton Conservatory
Alternative Parking:	Any street near the Park.
Hiking Time:	40 minutes
Length:	1.3 mile loop
Difficulty:	

Surface: Paved and mowed-grass paths

Trail Markings: Some signs

Uses:

Dogs: OK on leash

Admission: Free

Contact: Monroe County Parks Department
171 Reservoir Avenue, Rochester, NY 14620
(585) 256-4950

Highland Park was Monroe County's first public park, dedicated in 1890 to the children of Rochester. The park began as a dream of two nurserymen, George Ellwanger and Patrick Barry who donated 20 acres of their nursery grounds to the city. Famous for its collections of magnolia, horse chestnut, barberry, Japanese maple, rhododendron, and lilac (more than 1,200), Highland Park is one of the oldest public arboretums or "tree gardens" in the United States.

Here are the best times to view various flowering plants:

mid-April	forsythia
late-April	magnolia
early-May	tulip
mid-May	flowering dogwood
late-May	azalea, lilac, pansy bed, wisteria
early-June r	hododendron
July	hydrangea

While enjoying the park, don't miss the Lamberton Conservatory, a landmark in Highland Park since 1911. Within the glass walls of the Conservatory, located on Reservoir Drive, are a wonderful tropical forest area, exotic plants, desert plants, plants with economic uses such as banana and coffee trees, and seasonal floral displays. Exhibits are changed five times throughout the year. The Conservatory is open daily from 10 AM until 4 PM. Cost is $2/ person, with kids under 5 free.

The route described winds past the Highland Reservoir, and an overlook with a panoramic view of Rochester neighborhoods, then meanders downhill through the park. You'll pass the pansy bed then wind through the lilac grove. Numbered posts correspond to the descriptions below, giving you information on twenty varieties (within nine species) of lilacs. The final leg is uphill through the magnolia grove.

20. **Renoncule** (syringa vulgaris): This superior lilac is long-lived and bears large numbers of double lilac-colored flowers. One of the first developed by Victor Lemoine of France, the first horticulturist to cultivate lilacs.

19. **Rochester** (syringa vulgaris): Developed in Rochester, this was the first lilac to have more than four petals on a single floret (called radical doubling). The creamy-white flowers extend above dark-green glossy leaves.

18. **Primrose** (syringa vulgaris): Its outstanding pale-yellow color is not found in any other lilac. Developed in Holland in 1949.

17. **Hybrid** (syringa laciniata crossed with pinnatifolia): A cross between the Cutleaf lilac (#9) and the Pinnate lilac. The white flowers are flushed with purple and appear quite early. Notice the small, divided leaves.

16. **Znamya Lenina** (syringa vulgaris): Developed in Russia in 1963, one of the finest red-purple, single-flower lilacs.

15. **Frederick Law Olmsted** (syringa vulgaris): A Rochester hybrid named in 1987 after the designer of Highland Park. The abundant, single white flowers appear on a fairly dense shrub.

14. **Claude Bernard** (syringa hyacinthiflora): This Victor Lemoine selection blooms just before the common lilacs. The largest of the shrub lilacs, it produces double pinkish flowers with slightly twisted petals.

13. **President Lincoln** (syringa vulgaris): This hybrid was developed in 1916 by John Dunbar, the horticulturist who started Highland Park's lilac collection. It's one of the bluest lilacs, but new green foliage tends to hide the blossoms.

12. **Flower City** (syringa vulgaris): Developed in Rochester in 1983, has wonderful, single deep-purple blooms with numerous petals on a single flower. Underside of petals has a distinct silvery cast.

11. **Himalayan** (syringa emodi): Native to Afghanistan, this tall shrub has stout, gray branches and elliptical leaves.

10. **Cheyenne** (syringa oblata dilatata): Developed in 1971 and noted for its abundant, light-purple blooms and fine shrub shape. One of the few lilacs whose leaves turn orange in fall.

9. **Cutleaf** (syringa laciniata): A dense shrub native to northwestern China. Produces small, pale-purple tubular flowers early in May. The finely cut leaves are atypical of most lilacs.

8. **Rouen** (syringa chinensis): These large violet flower clusters produce a heavy fragrance that is most notable in high humidity. This flower is excellent for landscaping because it requires little maintenance.

7. **Corinne** (syringa vulgaris): A fine example of a magenta lilac, with somewhat open flower clusters. Developed in 1900 at the Baltet nursery in Troyes, France.

6. Mademoiselle Casimer Perrier (syringa vulgaris): A fine, white double flower developed in 1894 by Victor Lemoine.

5. Frau Wilhelm Pfitzer (syringa vulgaris): This large, vigorous lilac from Germany, produces clusters of very fragrant, single pink flowers.

4. Peking (syringa pekinensis): One of only two lilac species that are small trees. This variety is native to northern China. Huge clusters of tiny creamy-white flowers bloom in mid-June. The soft green foliage, draping branches, and reddish-brown bark make this an attractive tree throughout the year.

3. Handel (syringa prestoniae): A large, vigorous shrub with fragrant, tubular pink flowers. Blooms about two weeks later than most lilacs. Isabel Preston of Ottawa, Canada, bred it in 1935 for the rugged climate of Canadian prairies, crossing two species native to China.

2. Nokomis (syringa hyacinthiflora): The single lilac-colored flower blooms slightly before the majority of the collection. Shrub developed in 1934 by Frank Skinner of Manitoba, Canada.

1. Jessie Gardner (syringa vulgaris): This fine American lilac produces abundant clusters of brilliant violet flowers growing on a rather large, rounded shrub.

Trail Directions

• From Lamberton Conservatory, walk east along Reservoir Avenue until you reach the old stone reservoir building (Gate House No.2) at 0.3 mile.
• Turn right on the paved walkway and immediately pass a trail to the left.
• Bear left at the next junction and head away from the reservoir.
• Bear right at the circle and pass the overlook area.
• At 0.5 mile, head down a flight of stairs and bear right. (Straight is a good side trip to take if the azaleas and rhododendrons are in bloom.)
• Make a sharp left turn and head downhill.
• Follow the paved path as it winds downhill.
• Bear left at the next junction.
• At the base of the hill, just before Highland Avenue, turn right and head west on the grass, parallel to Highland Avenue.
• Pass the pansy bed and continue west along a grass path through the numbered lilac bushes.
• Turn right (NE) when you meet the paved walkway at 1.2 miles and head uphill.
• At the next junction turn left (N) and pass through the magnolia grove. This walkway will take you back to Reservoir Avenue.

Date Hiked: _____

Notes:

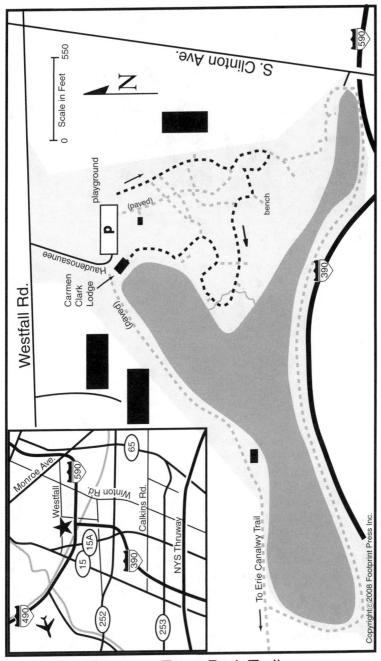

Brighton Town Park Trail

Brighton Town Park Trail

Location:	777 Westfall Road, Brighton. Immediately north of the I-390/I-590 intersection.
Directions:	Brighton Town Park entrance (Haudenosaunee Trail) is off Westfall Road, just west of South Clinton Avenue.
Alternative Parking:	None
Hiking Time:	25 minutes
Length:	0.5 mile loop (darkened trail) 1.2-mile loop around the pond
Difficulty:	👣 👣
Surface:	Dirt path
Trail Markings:	None
Uses:	🥾 🥾
Dogs:	OK on leash
Admission:	Free
Contact:	Brighton Recreation & Parks 220 Idlewood Road, Rochester, NY 14618 (585) 784-5260 www.townofbrighton.org/index.asp?NID=220

Step into this beech forest and the noisy, busy world outside will disappear. You'll forget that the intersections of two busy highways are less than 0.5 mile away. The calm, quiet and cool, shade will envelop your mind and body to wash away stress. Such is the magic of this urban oasis. Benches and large rocks can be found inside the woods, providing multiple resting points.

If you're up for a more strenuous jaunt, walk the 1.3 mile loop around the retention pond. The western leg is paved and leads to the Erie Canalway Trail. (Details in the Erie Canalway Trail can be found in *Take Your Bike - Family Rides in the Rochester Area*.) The eastern leg is not maintained but a well-trodden path through the mowed grass is available. Your serenade will be the whir of traffic overhead and the honking of ducks and geese who live on the pond.

Trail Directions

- From the parking area, head east across the grass toward the playground, passing a paved trail into the woods.
- Turn right (S) onto a wide path. This path will follow the edge of the woods for most of your walk.

264

A runner enjoys the Brighton Town Park Trail.

- Pass three trails to the right, then one trail to the left. (Left goes to a company parking lot.)
- Bear right at the next junction, staying in the woods.
  Note: To circumnavigate the pond, continue straight across open grass. Bear left around the end of the pond, then bear right between the pond and I-390. Continue following the pond's edge until you meet a paved path. Turn right and follow the paved path back to the main park area.
- Pass a path to the left which leads to a bench at woods edge.
- Pass two trails to the right.
- Pass three trails to the left which lead out of the woods.
- Pass two trails to the right.
- Follow the path to a picnic bench.
- Turn right and follow the pond walking across the grass, toward the lodge and parking lot.

Date Hiked: _____
Notes:

The pond in Brighton Town Park.

Turtles bask on a log in Brighton Town Park.

Definitions

Arboretum: A tree garden where a variety of trees are planted and labeled for study and enjoyment.

Battery box: A box housing a battery as backup power for the railroad crossing gates and flashing lights in case of a power outage.

Blaze: A rectangular swath of paint used on trees to mark the path of a trail.

Corduroy: A method of spanning a wet section of trail by laying logs perpendicular to the trail. This creates a bumpy effect like corduroy material.

Deciduous: Describes trees that lose their leaves in winter.

Derecho: A fast-moving, long-lived storm that produces winds in excess of 58 miles per hour over a path of at least 280 miles in length. Commonly called a micro-burst, this storm can quickly fell many trees.

Drumlin: An elongated or oval hill created from glacial debris.

Esker: A ridge of debris formed when a river flowed under the glacier in an icy tunnel. Rocky material accumulated on the tunnel beds, and when the glacier melted, a ridge of rubble remained.

Feeder: A diverted stream, brook, or other water source used to maintain water level in a canal.

Fulling mill: A mill for cleaning wool and producing cloth.

Gorp: An abbreviation for "good old raisins and peanuts." It is used today to cover any combination of snacks taken to eat while hiking.

Gristmill: A mill for grinding grain into flour.

Guard gates: Large metal or wood and metal barriers which can be lowered into the canal to stop the flow of water.

Marsh: An area of soft, wet land.

Meromictic lake: A very deep body of water surrounded by high ridges. Because the high ridges prevent the wind from blowing on the water, a motionless surface gives the lake a mirrored effect.

Mule: The sterile offspring of a male donkey and a female horse. Mules were often used to pull boats along the Erie Canal.

Oxbow: A U-shaped bend in a river which eventually gets cut-off from the main river and becomes a free-standing crescent shaped body of water.

Quonset hut:	A trademark used for a prefabricated portable hut having a semicircular roof of corrugated metal that curves down to form walls.
Riparian zone:	Land located on the bank of a natural waterway.
Sawmill:	A mill for cutting trees into lumber.
Swamp:	Wet, spongy land saturated and sometimes partially or intermittently covered with water.
Switchbacks:	Winding the trail back and forth across the face of a steep area to make the incline more gradual.
Trestle:	A framework consisting of vertical, slanted supports and horizontal crosspieces supporting a bridge. This construction is often used for railroad bridges.
Waste weir:	A dam along the side of the canal which allows overflow water to dissipate into a side waterway.

Trails 1.0 Mile or Less
(in shortest to longest order)

Trails 1.1 to 1.5 Miles
(in shortest to longest order)

Trails 1.6 to 2.3 Miles
(in shortest to longest order)

Trails 2.4 to 5.0 Miles
(in shortest to longest order)

Trails Longer Than 5 Miles
(in shortest to longest order)

Trails that Contain a Wheelchair Accessible Segment

1 Boot Trails

1 Boot Trails

2 Boot Trails

3 Boot Trails

3 Boot Trails

4 Boot Trails

Trails to Waterfalls

Educational Trails

Educational Trails

Historical Trails

Trails with a View

Trails with a Horticultural Flair

Trails to View Wildlife or Farm Animals

Trails for Horseback Riding

Trails for Bicycle Riding

Trails for Cross-country Skiing

Word Index

Word Index

Word Index

Word Index

Word Index

Word Index

Word Index

Word Index

About the Authors

The authors, Rich and Sue Freeman decided to make their living from what they love — hiking and bicycling. In 1996 they left corporate jobs to spend six months hiking 2,200 miles on the Appalachian Trail from Georgia to Maine. That adventure deepened their love of the outdoors and inspired them to share this love by

introducing others to the joys of hiking. Since most people don't have the option (let alone the desire) to undertake a six-month trek, they decided to focus on short hikes, near home. The result was the first edition (1997) of *Take A Hike! Family Walks in the Rochester Area.* They went on to explore hiking, bicycling and paddling trails throughout the Central and Western New York State region.

Rich and Sue continue to be active with various trail groups, and they enjoy doing trail work. In addition, their passion for long distance hiking continues. They have thru-hiked the 500-mile long Bruce Trail in Ontario, Canada, hiked across Spain on the Camino de Santiago Trail, hiked across England on the Coast to Coast Trail, and climbed Mt. Kilimanjaro in Africa. They have bicycled across New York State, following the Erie Canalway Trail and biked the C&O Canal Trail. Each year, in addition to doing guidebook research, they try to take at least one long adventure trip.

Since beginning their new career writing and publishing books, the Freemans' have pared down their living expenses and are enjoying a simpler lifestyle. They now have control of their own destiny and the freedom to head into the woods for a refreshing respite when the urge strikes. Still, their life is infinitely more cluttered than when they carried all their worldly needs on their backs for six months on the Appalachian Trail.

Other Books Available from Footprint Press, Inc.

Hiking:

200 Waterfalls in Central & Western New York - A Finders' Guide
ISBN#1-930480-01-6   U.S. $18.95
Discover over 200 wondrous waterfalls.

Peak Experiences – Hiking the Highest Summits in NY, County by County
ISBN# 0-9656974-01   U.S. $16.95
A guide to reaching the highest point in each county of New York State.

Take A Hike – Family Walks in New York's Finger Lakes Region
ISBN# 1-930480-20-2   U.S. $19.95
2nd edition - 68 day-hike trails in the Finger Lakes Region.

Bruce Trail – An Adventure Along the Niagara Escarpment
ISBN# 0-9656974-36   U.S. $16.95
Learn the secrets of backpackers on a five-week hike in Ontario, Canada, as they explore the abandoned Welland Canal routes, caves, ancient cedar forests, and white cobblestone beaches along Georgian Bay.

Backpacking Trails of Central & Western New York State
ISBN# none   U.S. $2.00
A 10-page booklet describing the backpackable trails of central and western NYS with contact information to obtain maps and trail guides.

Bird Watching:

Birding in Central & Western New York – Best Trails & Water Routes for Finding Birds
ISBN# 1-930480-00-8   U.S. $16.95
70 of the best places to spot birds on foot, from a car, or from a canoe.

Bicycling:

Take Your Bike! Family Rides in the Rochester Area
ISBN# 1-930480-02-4   U.S. $18.95
Converted railroad beds, paved bike paths and woods trails, combine to create the 42 safe bicycle adventures within an easy drive of Rochester, N.Y.

Take Your Bike! Family Rides in the Finger Lakes & Genesee Valley Region
ISBN# 0-9656974-44   U.S. $16.95
Converted railroad beds, woods trails, and little-used country roads combine to create the 40 safe bicycle adventures through central and western New York State.

Take Your Bike! Family Rides in New York's Finger Lakes Region
ISBN# 1-930480-22-9   U.S. $19.95
2nd edition - 43 bike trails in the Finger Lakes Region.

Explore History:

Cobblestone Quest - Road Tours of New York's Historic Buildings
ISBN# 1-930480-19-9   U.S. $19.95
17 self-guided tours for observing the history and diversity of unique cobblestone buildings that are found within a 65-mile radius of Rochester, NY, and nowhere else. Enjoy the tours by car, motorcycle, or bicycle.

Canoeing & Kayaking:

Take a Paddle - Western New York Quiet Water for Canoes & Kayaks
ISBN# 1-930480-23-7   U.S. $18.95
Offering over 250 miles of flat-water creeks and rivers, and 20 ponds and lakes, this guide provides a fun way to explore Western New York.

Take a Paddle - Finger Lakes New York Quiet Water for Canoes & Kayaks
ISBN# 1-930480-24-5   U.S. $18.95
Offering over 370 miles of flat-water creeks and rivers, and 35 ponds and lakes, this guide provides a fun way to explore the beautiful Finger Lakes region.

Self-help:

Alter – A Simple Path to Emotional Wellness
ISBN# 0-9656974-87   U.S. $16.95
A self-help manual that assists in recognizing and changing emotional blocks and limiting belief systems, using easy-to-learn techniques of biofeedback to retrieve subliminal information and achieve personal transformation.

For sample maps and chapters explore web site:
www.footprintpress.com

Yes, I'd like to order Footprint Press books:

\#

_____	*Take A Hike! Family Walks in NY's Finger Lakes*	$19.95
_____	*Take Your Bike! Family Rides in NY's Finger Lakes*	$19.95
_____	*200 Waterfalls in Central & Western NY*	$18.95
_____	*Take a Paddle - Western NY*	$18.95
_____	*Take a Paddle - Finger Lakes NY*	$18.95
_____	*Cobblestone Quest*	$19.95
_____	*Peak Experiences—Hiking the Highest Summits of NY*	$16.95
_____	*NYS County Summit Club patch*	$2.00
_____	*Birdng in Central & Western NY*	$16.95
_____	*Take A Hike! Family Walks in the Rochester Area*	$19.95
_____	*Take Your Bike! Family Rides in the Rochester Area*	$18.95
_____	*Take Your Bike! Family Rides in the Finger Lakes & Genesee Valley*	$16.95
_____	*Bruce Trail—Adventure Along the Niagara Escarpment*	$16.95
_____	*Backpacking Trails of Central & Western NYS*	$2.00
_____	*Alter—A Simple Path to Emotional Wellness*	$16.95

Sub-total: $_____

FL State and Canadian residents add 7% tax: $_____

Shipping & handling: $ 3.50

Total enclosed: $_____

Your Name: _____

Address: _____

City: _____ State (Province): _____

Zip (Postal Code): _____ Country: _____

Make check payable and mail to:

Footprint Press, Inc.
303 Pine Glen Court, Englewood, FL 34223

Or order through web site: **www.footprintpress.com**